A Taste of Honey

GCSE Student Guide

Methuen Drama publications for GCSE students

Available and forthcoming

GCSE Student Editions

Willy Russell's *Blood Brothers*
Simon Stephens's *The Curious Incident of the Dog in the Night-Time*
Charlotte Keatley's *My Mother Said I Never Should*
Shelagh Delaney's *A Taste of Honey*

GCSE Student Guides

Willy Russell's *Blood Brothers* by Ros Merkin
Simon Stephens's *The Curious Incident of the Dog in the Night-Time* by Jacqueline Bolton
Dennis Kelly's *DNA* by Maggie Inchley
Alan Bennett's *The History Boys* by Steve Nicholson
J. B. Priestley's *An Inspector Calls* by Philip Roberts
R. C. Sherriff's *Journey's End* by Andrew Maunder
Charlotte Keatley's *My Mother Said I Never Should* by Sophie Bush
Shelagh Delaney's *A Taste of Honey* by Kate Whittaker

A Taste of Honey

GCSE Student Guide

KATE WHITTAKER

Series Editor: Jenny Stevens

Bloomsbury Methuen Drama
An imprint of Bloomsbury Publishing Plc

B L O O M S B U R Y
LONDON · OXFORD · NEW YORK · NEW DELHI · SYDNEY

Bloomsbury Methuen Drama

An imprint of Bloomsbury Publishing Plc

Imprint previously known as Methuen Drama

50 Bedford Square	1385 Broadway
London	New York
WC1B 3DP	NY 10018
UK	USA

www.bloomsbury.com

BLOOMSBURY, METHUEN DRAMA and the Diana logo are trademarks of Bloomsbury Publishing Plc

British Library Cataloguing-in-Publication Data
A catalogue record for this book is available from the British Library.

ISBN:	PB:	978-1-4742-2971-5
	ePDF:	978-1-4742-2972-2
	epub:	978-1-4742-2973-9

Library of Congress Cataloging-in-Publication Data
A catalog record for this book is available from the Library of Congress

Series: GCSE Student Guides

Typeset by RefineCatch Limited, Bungay, Suffolk
Printed and bound in Great Britain

CONTENTS

ACKNOWLEDGEMENTS

Sincere thanks to Bijan Sheibani, Sally Lindsay and Krista Carson for their invaluable contributions, and the warmth and generosity with which they made them. I am indebted to my wonderful colleagues at Birmingham City University for their support, and to my inspiring students, past and present.

This book is dedicated to my parents, and to Martin, a boy from Manchester. I will forever fail to thank you enough.

CHAPTER ONE

The Play

Introduction

Reading a play

A play is different from a novel, short story or poem. Unlike these other types of literature, it is drama: written to be performed on a stage, by actors, with an audience watching. Because of this, the copy of *A Taste of Honey* that you may have on your desk is a bit like an architect's blueprint for a house. A blueprint shows how the house should look when it is built; the play text tells the reader how it should look and sound when it is produced on a stage. From this information, it is possible to imagine the mood and atmosphere of the play in performance, and the effect that these could have on a live audience. As a piece of writing, therefore, a play is a set of instructions. It allows the playwright (author) to communicate their ideas to theatre directors, designers and actors. It is not complete 'on the page', like a novel; it is complete 'on the stage', whenever it is being performed.

No two productions of a play are ever exactly the same because its 'instructions' will be interpreted differently by different people. There is no 'correct' way to perform any one play, but various possible interpretations. Some will be more effective than others, of course! A good way to appreciate the importance of interpretation to drama is to do an online image search of performances of a very famous play – for example, by Shakespeare – and compare and contrast what you find. Details about different productions of *A Taste of Honey* are contained in this book.

To read a play effectively

1 Read it in one go, with a break halfway through. This will give you some idea of what a performance would be like.

2 Read it out loud. This is best with a different person reading each character, and one person reading the stage directions.

3 Select important scenes and try acting them out, or think about how you would direct them.

4 Look at online images and video footage of past productions.

5 Note any moments that you think might have a more powerful effect on an audience member than on a reader, using the following word bank:

Shocking   Humorous   Violent   Painful   Upsetting
Uplifting   Frustrating   Emotive   Embarrassing

Try to avoid these common mistakes

1 Ignoring stage directions, and only reading the dialogue (lines that are spoken in performance). Stage directions contain crucial instructions not just about *what* happens, but *how* it happens. They also convey information about themes and characters.

2 Thinking that drama is the same as film or television. If you watch a programme or film more than once, it will be exactly the same every time, whereas no two performances of a play are ever identical: even in the same theatre with the same actors. It is only with

drama that the people performing are in the same space as the people watching, and the two groups aware of one another.

3 Using the words 'book' or 'novel' to refer to a play. The terms play and drama can be used to mean both the hard copy that you will read and study, and any performance of it.

Terms

Although Jo's boyfriend's name is Jimmie, Delaney calls the character 'Boy.' He is therefore referred to as 'Boy' throughout this book.

The National Theatre staged *A Taste of Honey* in 2014, and the production was accompanied by a Background Pack which is available to download online at: http://www.nationaltheatre. org.uk/document/a-taste-of-honey-background-pack. References are made to this pack in this book.

Geography

The play's setting, Salford, has been part of the county of Greater Manchester since 1974; in 1958, when the play was written, Salford was in Lancashire. Jo's description of the flat as a 'Manchester maisonette' (77) reflects a common perception of Salford as part of the larger, neighbouring city. However, Salford is also a city itself.

Overview

Act one, scene one

The play's first scene introduces the two central characters: single, working-class mother, Helen, and her fifteen year-old daughter, Jo. They are moving into a 'comfortless flat' (29) in

Salford on a cold, rainy day in December. Helen has little money, which is represented visually as well as through dialogue: the main part of the set is the interior of the flat. Spoken references to its dismal location reinforce the characters' poverty.

Helen drinks whisky and behaves in a self-centred, demanding way. Jo acts resentfully towards her mother – whom she calls 'Helen' (30) – and says that she will soon be leaving school in order to get a job and move out. The audience learn that Helen has forced Jo to move house numerous times. Helen finds and compliments drawings of Jo's that she did not know existed, which shows Jo's creativity and Helen's lack of knowledge about her. The emotional distance between them is at odds with their physical closeness; Jo observes that they will be 'sharing a bed again' (30).

Helen's ex-boyfriend, Peter, arrives at the flat unexpectedly. He is a wealthy, 'brash car salesman' (39) and, by using a business metaphor to describe his past relationship with Helen, hints at her living as a 'semi-whore' (29): not a prostitute, but a woman who lives off her boyfriends in part. Ten years older than him, Helen does not accept directly when Peter proposes, but hints to Jo later that she might be getting married for a second time. The scene ends with Jo expressing her fear of the dark 'inside houses' (47), highlighting her negative feelings about families.

Act one, scene two

At the opening of Scene Two only, the action unfolds '*on the street*' (47) outside the flat. It features Jo and her sailor boyfriend, Boy, and is set a week or two after Scene One. Jo shrugs off his concerns about people's reactions (including Helen's) to the fact he is black, and accepts his proposal of marriage.[1] As it is too big for her finger, she puts the engagement ring on a string to wear around her neck and they decide to get

---

[1] You can read about attitudes to interracial relationships in the 1950s under 'Contexts'.

married in six months, when Boy is next on leave from the Navy. Jo tells him that she is about to start work in a bar.

Immediately afterwards, Jo enters the flat and Helen announces that she is marrying Peter. This part of the scene contains a key monologue of Helen's, in which she advises Jo to take control of her life, yet demonstrates a belief in fate. Peter arrives, and Jo is hostile to both of them; Helen moves between defending her daughter and defending her fiancé against the other's unpleasant comments. Despite her remarks, Jo does not wish to be left alone, and cries when Helen and Peter leave to go on an early honeymoon to Blackpool.

Boy appears, finds Jo upset, and prepares her a 'cold cure' (64) to drink. Unlike Helen, he is warm and caring, and accepts Jo's invitation to stay over Christmas. Jo voices her belief that this will be the last time they will spend together.

The end of Scene Two sees Helen return for her wedding. It is now after Christmas and Boy has left the flat. Jo confesses to being engaged when Helen notices her ring; Helen's angry reaction shows real concern for Jo. Already knowing that she was conceived during an extra-marital affair, Jo asks about her father and is reluctant to believe Helen's claim that he was 'a bit – retarded' (73). Helen also reveals that this was her first sexual experience, and a one-off encounter 'that lasted five minutes' (73). She leaves to marry Peter.

Act two, scene one

It is June of the following year. Jo, visibly pregnant, has befriended a young art student called Geof, and has two jobs to pay the rent in Helen's absence. Geof's homosexuality is strongly suggested: he is offended when Jo teasingly asks him about it and insinuates that this is the reason he has been evicted by his landlady.[2] Geof accepts the offer to sleep on the

---

[2] Male homosexuality was illegal at this time. In 'Contexts', this is looked at in more depth.

sofa and advises Jo to tell Helen about the pregnancy, although they have had no contact since the wedding day. Jo claims to know nothing other the fact that Helen now lives in 'a big, white house somewhere' (81). Geof and Jo recite nursery rhymes, and Jo invents fantasies about Boy. Although six months have passed and he has not returned, she is content with daydreams about him.

It is 'a month or two later' (86). Miserable in the summer heat, Jo expresses bitter disinterest in motherhood; Geof, who likes babies, encourages her to embrace it. His love for Jo is shown by practical support (like making baby clothes), and romantic gestures: an awkward kiss and a marriage proposal. Jo does not welcome either, but comforts Geof, and agrees that they should carry on living together.

Helen arrives and asks questions about Jo's pregnancy. Her aggressive manner leads to both women becoming angry, and Helen chasing Jo around the flat. Geof comes under attack from the pair: Helen insults him, using homophobic slang, and Jo is angry because she realizes he must have told Helen about her pregnancy. The arrival of Peter, drunk, heightens the chaotic mood and shows that his marriage to Helen is deteriorating. He echoes Helen by insulting Jo and Geof, and shows off about an affair he has had. Jo refuses Helen's means of support – money and a room in her house – which is withdrawn by Peter, in any case; he takes the money that Helen brought for Jo as he leaves. Helen follows him after Jo rejects her offer to stay.

Act two, scene two

Jo's first line indicates that her baby is nearly due, so the audience know that it is now September. Geof continues to look after Jo, and reassures her that Helen was exaggerating about her father's mental deficiencies. Jo violently rejects the baby doll that he gives her for 'practice', symbolizing her negative feelings about becoming a mother. In the calmer atmosphere that follows, the pair prepare to have tea and cake, content in one another's company.

Helen arrives with all her possessions, as at the beginning. She brings presents for Jo, and is friendly and attentive; to Geof, her rudeness continues. Helen admits that Peter has 'thrown [her] out' (117), and pressures Geof into leaving for good. Jo goes into labour and is comforted by Helen, through whom Delaney creates dramatic irony: Helen allows Jo to believe that Geof's absence is only temporary. Helen is horrified when Jo tells her that her baby 'may be black' (124), and goes to the pub. Alone, Jo repeats one of the nursery rhymes that Geof recited on the day he moved into the flat.

Things to do

A plot is made up of what happens in a play. Write a summary of the play's plot in a maximum of 150 words. As a class, discuss what you decided to include, what to leave out, and why. What are the most important parts of the plot?

Contexts

Production history

1958	Premiere performance by the Theatre Workshop at the Theatre Royal, Stratford, London, directed by Joan Littlewood.[3]
1959	Transferred to Wyndham's Theatre in London's West End.
1960	Second production opened on Broadway, New York.
1961	Broadway production won the New York Drama Critics' Circle Award. Film version released.
1981	A New York revival.
1989	Staged at the Royal Exchange, Manchester.

---

[3] This theatre is now called the Theatre Royal Stratford East.

1990s	Various British productions, including those by English Touring Theatre (1993) and the Bristol Old Vic (1996–7 season).
2000	Selected for the National Theatre's list of *100 Plays of the Century* (available online).
2004	Broadcast of an adaptation on BBC Radio 3.
2005–2015	Produced in numerous theatres during the decade in which it turned fifty (2008): Sheffield Crucible (2006 and 2012); the Lowry, Salford (2007); Manchester's Royal Exchange (2008), and the Royal Lyceum, Edinburgh (2013). In 2014, key productions included the National Theatre (London) and Hull Truck Theatre (Yorkshire).

Britain in the 1950s

Social class is mentioned in this section as the concept of 'working-class' is especially relevant to the play. This table outlines *typical* features of three key social classes in the 1950s. You may wish to refer back to it during your studies.

Category:	Working-class	Middle-class	Upper-class
Housing	Rented, low-quality property	Rented or bought property	Inherited property
Education	School (leaving age: fifteen)	College or university*	Fee-paying public school; Oxford or Cambridge university*
Employment	Manual labour (servant, factory worker)	Teacher, doctor or office worker*	Judge, high-ranking politician, or aristocrat*

*In these fields, women were marginalized or excluded completely.

After the horrors of World War Two (1939–45), the 1950s was an optimistic period. Queen Elizabeth II came to the throne in 1952, which represented a positive new beginning for many. The Welfare State, developed in the 1940s, meant the government took responsibility for people's wellbeing. The National Health Service and free secondary education are two elements of the State that still exist, along with social security (represented in the play through Helen's question about 'maternity benefit' [98]). Wartime food rationing ended in 1954, and most adults had jobs. Household items such as televisions because affordable, and there was an increase in the sale of cars. As people earned more, the British middle-class swelled. Britain had had a rigid class system – in which a person's 'position' in society was unlikely to change – so this was an important development. With his job as a car salesman, the character of Peter represents those who achieved a higher social status through making money. More jobs meant that young people could also earn a wage. The play captures the connection between financial and personal freedom through Jo. For her, employment means independence from Helen. In 1957, the Conservative prime minister Harold Macmillan famously said that 'most of our people have never had it so good'.

However, Britain still faced problems. It had become a wealthy, leading power in the world through being an Empire. This meant forcibly ruling poorer countries in places that included the Indian subcontinent, the Caribbean and Africa. After the war, Britain could not afford its Empire. Its problems were exacerbated by rebellions in several countries under its rule, including the Mau Mau Uprising in Kenya that began in 1952, to which Jo refers in the play. Uprisings were a step towards certain of these countries becoming independent. The end of the Empire meant an enormous loss of power and status for Britain. Furthermore, it was involved in the 'arms race', developing nuclear weapons, which furthered the financial strain.

In the country itself, 'economic benefits [were] not equally distributed: the north of Britain [lagged] behind the south'

(Pattie 2012: 18). Salford, the play's northern setting, had been one of the poorest areas in the country in the 1930s. Like Manchester, it was bombed during the war, so – despite post-war rebuilding projects – a lack of adequate housing affected many. *Honey* represents the limited choices available to the less well-off through its set and dialogue. When Peter claims that 'Nobody could live in a place like this', Jo responds: 'Only about fifty thousand people' (41).

Jo's outspokenness, shown here, relates to another part of 1950s Britain: the teenager. Before this decade, people were treated as *either* children or adults. The idea of an 'in-between' period in which young people claimed the right to self-expression – often rejecting older generations' views – was new. Rebellious Teddy Boys (or 'Teds') were gangs of young men whose name stemmed from their Edwardian-style fashions; they became associated with alcohol and violent behaviour. Jo calls Geof a 'proper Ted' as a joke: he is not rebellious, but old-fashioned, or 'a *real* Edwardian' (105, my emphasis). Theatre critic Michael Billington has argued that 'age [. . .] was the dividing factor' in Britain during this time (Billington 2007: 84). This emphasizes the significance of 'the teenager', but is also relevant to changes that were happening in British theatre.

Theatre in the 1950s

During this decade, 'theatre [reflected] a society in transition' (Pattie 2012: 4). On the one hand, there were dramas such as Terence Rattigan's *Variations on a Theme* (1958) that – like pre-war plays by the writer Noël Coward – focused on the personal lives of upper-class people and were set in beautiful hotels or drawing rooms. On the other hand, a so-called 'New Wave' of young writers did something new by portraying ordinary, everyday experience, including that of working-class people. This challenged a tradition in which the lower classes either did not appear in plays, or were presented as stereotypes.

John Osborne's *Look Back in Anger* (1956) is considered the first play of the New Wave: 'the landmark between the old and the new' (Eyre and Wright 2000: 236). It features a middle-class man, Jimmy Porter, who resents the upper-class world of privilege represented by his wife Alison. The action is set in a basic attic flat and opens with Alison ironing. This would have been a very unusual sight for a 1950s audience. A focus on the unglamorous details of home and family life gave rise to the term 'kitchen sink drama'. *Honey* falls into this category.

Osborne, and other playwrights like John Arden, became known as 'Angry Young Men' because their work attacked a lingering, old-fashioned class system that showed there were still inequalities in British society, despite the changes of the post-war years. The 'Angry Young Men', which also included novelists like Kingsley Amis, criticized the new consumer culture – in which people took pleasure in buying material goods like televisions – for being shallow and meaningless.

A Taste of Honey *in context*

As part of the New Wave, *A Taste of Honey* was radical, which means an extreme version of what is acceptable. Delaney has been described as an 'Angry Young Woman' by various journalists and other writers, yet her focus was somewhat different from Osborne and Arden's. Regarding social class, Delaney's quick-witted characters reflect a comment she made in an interview:

> I had strong ideas about what I wanted to see in the theatre. [. . .] Usually [working-class] North country people are shown as gormless, whereas in actual fact they are very alive and cynical.

> Delaney in Kitchin 1960: 177

The working-class was not the only group not represented (or not represented fairly) in plays, and oppressed in reality. In terms of 1950s society, 'increased comfort [masked] other, more painful realities (such as the status of women [. . .], racism [. . .], and the [. . .] action fought [. . .] against the decriminalisation of homosexuality)' (Pattie 2012: 19). Delaney portrayed themes about these 'realities' of prejudice and inequality. *If* she was 'angry' – and it is only possible to speculate about this, through analysing the play – it was about these issues.

Honey's lead characters are female, working-class, and, by Act Two, a single mother and single mother-to-be. During the war, women had done men's jobs such as manual work in factories. A drive to re-connect women with their traditional roles in the home and family occurred once war was over. Apart from widows, unmarried mothers were seen as a 'disgrace' and treated as 'second-class citizens' (Ince 2014: 17). Extra-marital sex and female sexual desire were taboo; women were expected to look attractive for (potential) husbands, and be selfless wives and mothers. One of the reasons *Honey* is radical is because Helen and Jo deviate from these standards.

An explanation given for why Delaney wrote the play was that she had seen *Variations on a Theme* and 'thought she could do better herself' (Taylor 1963 [1962]: 112); in part, because she was unimpressed by the portrayal of a gay male character. Homosexuality was illegal in the fifties, and there were strict restrictions on playwrights including it in their work, either through themes or characters.[4] All scripts for professional productions had to be approved by the Lord Chamberlain's Office (a board of censors). The fact that *Honey* was permitted, despite offending some of the censors, shows this was a time of change. In September 1957, a document called the Wolfenden Report advised the government that homosexuality should no longer be a crime. Although this did not come to be until 1967, the Lord Chamberlain relaxed the rules about homosexuality in plays in 1958.

Ideas about race also made the play radical. As the Empire collapsed, Britain saw mass immigration of black and Asian

---

[4] All references to homosexuality in this book are about men.

people from countries it had ruled. Racial abuse of immigrants, and those from (racial) minority groups, was common. Tensions between black and white communities resulted in violent riots in Nottingham and London's Notting Hill in 1958, just months after *Honey* premiered. In Nottingham, fighting erupted because a mixed-race couple – a black man and a white woman – were seen together in a pub. Unsurprisingly, given this context, mixed-race families were regarded with disgust.[5] This shows how ground-breaking it was to portray a likeable black character, and an interracial relationship, at this time.

The 1950s was also 'a time when women's voices were virtually unheard in the British theatre' (Billington 2007: 111). Apart from Delaney, Ann Jellicoe and Joan Littlewood were two key female figures in this male-dominated context. Jellicoe, a playwright, wrote *The Sport of My Mad Mother* (1958), also about motherhood. Joan Littlewood, one of the most significant British theatre directors of the twentieth century, directed the premiere of *Honey*. Her importance to the play was highlighted by Delaney in a television interview.[6] Both Littlewood and Delaney were working-class women; *Honey* is radical for this reason, as well as for its themes and characters. It can be described as a feminist play because it challenged the way society marginalized both *real* women working in theatre, and fictional women represented *through* theatre (characters).

Things to do

1 Find out more about one event or trend of this period, such as the race riots. Write a monologue from the point of view of someone who was there.

---

[5] First-hand accounts of women with mixed-raced children are documented in the National Theatre Background Pack (see 'Overview').

[6] This short 1959 ITN interview with Delaney is available online at: https://www.youtube.com/watch?v=SM22loR53TQ.

2 Create a poster that shows two sides of the 1950s: as a time of prosperity for some, and a time of hardship for others.

3 Create a collage entitled 'Delaney's Salford' to represent *Honey*'s setting. To prepare, find descriptions of the location in the play.

4 Find images of some of the plays mentioned in this section. This could include photographs of performances, production posters and front covers of play texts. In pairs, discuss what these images suggest about the 'new' theatre of the 1950s.

5 Do an online image search of women in British adverts of the 1950s and make a list of words or phrases to describe them. How are Jo and Helen different or similar?

A Taste of Honey *today*

The position of women has changed enormously since the 1950s. However, most of the plays staged in professional theatres are still male-authored, and it is a minority that take female experiences as their main focus. Fewer than twenty female playwrights appear on the National Theatre's list, *100 Plays of the Twentieth Century*, and in 2013, only 31 per cent of the (professional) plays produced in Britain were written by women.[7] *Honey* is not unusual, as it was in 1958, but plays by *and* about women are still not hugely common. For this reason, it is still a feminist text.

---

[7] This statistic was in a report about women playwrights, available online in theatre publication *The Stage*: https://www.thestage.co.uk/news/2015/less-third-new-plays-written-women-report-finds/.

Interracial relationships and homosexuality are no longer taboo in drama; the Theatre Act (1968) ended the Lord Chamberlain's power to ban plays. However, there are elements of *Honey* that could prove *more* shocking for a contemporary audience than for one of the 1950s, such as Jo being given alcohol and cigarettes by Helen and Peter. Laws about drinking were more relaxed before the 1964 Licensing Act, and it was only in 1957 that the Medical Research Council confirmed the link between smoking and lung cancer. In the 'Behind the Scenes' interview with Sally Lindsay, who played Helen in 2008 at Manchester's Royal Exchange, you can read about how audience members' negative reaction to racism affected the way the play was performed. This particular production also included an aspect of Manchester's culture from a period after the 1950s: the music of 1980s band, The Smiths, who have used lines of Delaney's in their songs, and images of her for album artwork. These things show how a drama written decades ago will be staged and perceived differently in the present.

Themes

A Taste of Honey

The title is a figure of speech, so its meaning is not literal. Rather, this is a metaphor for the theme of short-lived, happy experiences. The phrase 'a taste of honey' comes from the Bible (the Book of Samuel). Jonathan, the son of Saul, ate some honey when he was supposed to be fasting, and was punished by being threatened with death. Each metaphorical 'taste of honey' in the play similarly results in a sort of 'punishment': Jo's relationship with Boy ends in an unwanted pregnancy, for instance. The 'tastes' in the play, experienced by the female characters first and foremost, are breaks from the challenges of their everyday lives. Other, specific examples of this theme are contained in the next section ('Character').

Things to do

1 Write down two or three of your own 'tastes of honey':
  a great holiday, or just five minutes of laughing
  uncontrollably with a friend. (Unlike the characters, your
  experiences do not have to have ended badly!) Share one
  of your memories with a classmate. Do you think good
  experiences are made more special by being short-term
  or unusual?

2 Devise a new title for the play (something original, or a
  quotation from another text). Aim to make it
  metaphorical, and describe a key theme.

Women's roles and motherhood

Traditional ideas about women are challenged by this play.
The theme of motherhood is key to this. Both female characters
do not match up to the post-war model of an 'ideal' mother,
who behaves in a selflessly committed, caring and domesticated
way. (If you have completed activity 5 on page 14 in the
'Contexts' section, see if you can make any links between these
'ideals' and your thoughts about 1950s advertising.)

The female characters' lack of maternal 'instinct' suggests
that being a woman does not mean being suited to motherhood.
This is one of the reasons that the play has a feminist element.
It opposes the idea that because of her biology (being
anatomically female), a woman will behave according to
traditional standards set for her by society. There are close
connections between a person's biological sex, and society's
expectations of their behaviour based on that sex, especially
when the play was first produced. This is emphasized by Jo's
line – 'I don't want to be a mother. I don't want to be a woman'
(75) – in which the similarity between the two sentences

highlights how society perceives being a mother as a key part of being female.[8] The play's challenge to 'ideals' of motherhood is one way it questions women's roles more broadly.

As with Helen's treatment of Jo, Jo's own attitude to becoming a mother is unmaternal. When Geof gives her a toy doll on which to 'practise', her reaction is to '*Suddenly and violently [fling] the doll to the ground*', claiming 'I'll bash its brains out' (111). Jo's action symbolizes her rejection of motherhood. In the previous scene, a physical rejection of motherhood is represented through speech when Jo hints that Helen has had abortions in the past.

The female characters' neglectfulness and selfish tendencies are part of the theme of unconventional motherhood. It is established that Helen abandoned Jo throughout her childhood; when she leaves to go on holiday with Peter, the act of neglect is reinforced by differences between her and Jo. Helen appears in her 'best' hat, and is told by Peter that she looks 'utterly fantastic' (61–2) before refusing Jo money for a 'new dress' (63). The other significant point at which Helen abandons Jo, her selfishness is emphasized by the fact that Jo is vulnerable, in labour.

Jo's own neglectfulness is shown symbolically. During the first scene, she states her plan to plant flower bulbs; in Act Two, Geof discovers them dead. This represents Jo's unsuitability to a maternal, caring role. Like Helen, her instinct is for *self*-preservation, not the selflessness of an 'ideal' mother.

Despite all this elements, the theme of motherhood is depicted more traditionally at points. In particular, the concern that Helen shows for Jo reflects a side of her that 'hankers after conventions' (Wandor 2001: 61). Her angry reaction to Jo's engagement contrasts with the more casual bickering of earlier scenes, revealing genuine frustration and worry. Jo's pregnancy, too, is a catalyst for maternal behaviour from Helen. There are

---

[8] You can see this moment being performed by Rebecca Ryan, a minute into the trailer for the 2013 production at the Royal Lyceum in Edinburgh, available online at: https://vimeo.com/57050765.

explosive exchanges between mother and daughter in Act Two, Scene One, but Helen's reason for visiting the flat is to offer Jo support; she does not remain, without Peter, because Jo rejects her. The calmer mood of the final scene stems from Helen being at her most caring, calling Jo 'love' (114) and reassuring her about labour pains. Jo's criticism of Helen's 'mother-love act' (98) in the first half of the second act – as something that has come too late – highlights that this is unusual behaviour.

Aside from motherhood, Jo and Helen differ from mainstream standards of womanhood in other ways, such as lacking domestic skills and having sexual appetites. (Although 1950s women were under pressure to be attractive, expressions of their *own* desires were generally taboo.) Very little of the action involves the women being in the kitchen of the flat. This is worth noting as kitchens are associated with conventional women's roles, like cooking for a family. Both Jo and Helen do appear in, or on, the bed. This visual feature, like Jo's pregnancy, reinforces that female characters are (or become) sexually active. Connections between the set and the women are looked at further under 'Dramatic technique'.

Geof is important to the theme of motherhood as a male character who is more maternal than either of the female ones. In Helen's absence, he becomes a replacement mother figure to Jo and her unborn child. More broadly, Geof occupies a traditional female role through doing domestic tasks (including baking, which associates him with the kitchen). Just as women, in this play, do not have the skills or 'instincts' traditionally associated with them, men are not incapable of maternal and domestic behaviour. The presentation of Boy reinforces this, as he takes care of Jo, and used to be a nurse (a traditionally female job).

The motherhood theme is also represented through the dialogue and stage directions about local children, outside the flat. In particular, the repeated sound of children singing in Act Two, Scene One creates the sense that they are all around Jo, who cannot ignore or escape them. This reflects how she is trapped in her position of expectant mother.

Things to do

1 '1950s "ideals" about women's roles still exist.'

   Prepare a short group presentation to share your point of view about this statement. Draw on your own observations, and media articles and images.

2 In pairs, select three quotations not mentioned in this section that you think best reflect Helen's non-maternal attitude. Write a paragraph about this theme, using your quotations as evidence.

Maternal relationships

Closely related to the theme above, maternal relationships are represented through Helen and Jo. Jo is important to the play's portrayal of maternal bonds as a daughter, as well as a mother-to-be. The non-traditional quality of the women's relationship reinforces how they are portrayed to rebel against 'ideals' of female behaviour.

The emotional distance between the two is established at the start, in part through language: Jo calls her mother 'Helen' (30), and Helen makes negative comments about Jo in the third person, such as: '*She*'s not got a bit of consideration in her' (34, my emphasis). The fact that Jo does not call Helen 'mother' hints to the audience that she is an inadequate parent before the action confirms it.

The hurling of insults and criticisms is central to the women's relationship and Helen's non-maternal manner. Jo's lack of respect reflects the rise of the teenager as a rebellious presence in 1950s Britain. Her behaviour differs from that expected of earlier generations, as this exchange shows:

Helen   [. . .] Go and see if that kettle's boiling.
Jo   See yourself. [. . .]

> **Helen**   See yourself! [. . .] I would never have dared talk to
> my mother like that when I was your age. She'd have
> knocked me into the middle of next week. (34–5)

Jo's attitude to her mother is often resentful and accusatory.
However, her insults are a sort of verbal self-defence, as when
Helen becomes angry about her pregnancy:

> **Helen**   You know what they're calling you round here? A
> silly little whore!
> **Jo**   Well, they all know where I get it from, too. (96)

Helen does not just criticize and attack Jo (and threaten to
attack her physically), but fails to nurture her through praise.
Her one compliment, of Jo's artistic skills, is undermined by a
sly insult; she wonders where one of the drawings would be
'least noticeable' (37) if she put it on the wall. At points, Jo
makes positive claims about herself, such as stating that she is
'too young and beautiful' (36) to get married. This is a means
of compensation: Helen rarely praises her, so she has to 'praise'
herself. Displays of *apparent* confidence are a way she copes
with being neglected. The fact that Jo is actually insecure is
explored under 'Character'; in 'Behind the Scenes', actor Sally
Lindsay comments on the damaging effect Helen has on Jo's
confidence.

Blame features, too, as part of the maternal relationship.
Aside from criticizing Helen's parenting directly, Jo also re-
directs her frustrations, such as when she sees an unwashed
boy from the window, and says of his mother: 'Think of all the
harm she does, having children' (86). Helen blames Jo for her
first husband's decision to divorce her. Therefore, the end of
her marriage is shown to be a reason for Helen's poor treatment
of Jo. One outcome of their strained relationship is Helen's
limited knowledge of her daughter's life: her drawings,
engagement and pregnancy are all important things that Helen
finds out about without Jo's wanting to tell her. As with her
verbal retorts, and attempts to appear self-confident, Jo's

guarded attitude in personal matters depicts a non-traditional mother–daughter relationship.

Food and drink feature symbolically. Milk symbolizes motherhood, because of breastfeeding: something that nurtures, and creates a bond between mother and child. Jo's hatred of milk, and (repeated) refusal to drink it, shows the troubled nature of her relationship with Helen, and desire to resist the bond between them. Given the association between maternity and the feeding of a child, it is significant that Helen is the only character who does not offer Jo sustenance in some way. This furthers her untraditional qualities, reflected in Act One when she refuses to cook for Jo:

> **Jo**   You should prepare my meals like a proper mother.
> **Helen**   When have I ever laid claim to being a proper mother? (63)

Boy and Geof each encourage Jo to drink milk, at two points when she is physically and emotionally weak; the contrast between their behaviour and Helen's heightens her neglectfulness. Alcohol and cigarettes are the only (consumable) items that she does give Jo. These are sources of escapism that do physical harm, and cannot nurture, symbolizing how Helen resists her role in the maternal relationship. At the same time, her actions are not meant to be damaging, but supportive. Helen, as a mother, is more inept than spiteful.

With its connection to breastfeeding, the symbol of milk represents the biological bond between Helen and Jo. It is important to be aware that this bond does exist, *and* that both characters try to strengthen it at points. This makes the theme of maternal relationships more complicated, as the play challenges traditional ideas about the connection between mother and daughter, but also shows a maternal bond that is strong and hard to escape. Jo and Helen's shared bed jars with the emotional gulf between them, yet also symbolizes their interdependent relationship. They are further presented as interdependent through sharing handkerchiefs, and in their reactions to each of the male character's impact upon their relationship. Peter and Geof come between the women – Jo is jealous of Peter, and Helen, of Geof – while the outcome of Boy's relationship with Jo makes Helen behave maternally.

The banter and repartee between mother and daughter further shows that the theme of maternal relationships is not one-dimensional. Although Jo and Helen distance themselves from each another through language, their duologues also strengthen their bond: Helen tells Geof that they 'enjoy' (97) arguing. In performance, parts of the women's fast-paced duologues would be humorous, creating a light-hearted atmosphere. This effect means that an audience would not *only* see Jo and Helen's relationship as difficult, or even depressing, despite the fact that it is challenging and non-traditional.

Things to do

1 In groups, select two short passages from the play, one that shows the unconventional nature of Helen and Jo's relationship, and one that shows their bond or an example of Helen caring for Jo. Rehearse and perform the extracts for your classmates, who should comment on the difference between them. Alternatively, present a prepared reading of your extracts.

2 Write a short scene between Jo and Geoff set just after Helen leaves in Act Two, Scene One. The first line should include the words 'the famous mother-love act'. Lay out your scene as a play script and include stage directions.

Families, marriage and sex

As shown in terms of motherhood, characters in the play do not properly fit their traditional positions within a family. The play's challenge to 'ideals' of motherhood is, therefore, part of the way it questions traditional family structures. A surrogate or replacement figure is often better at performing a role than the person expected to do it, such as Geof being a better 'mother' than Helen.

Helen's failings are not only emphasized by Geof (and, to a lesser extent, Boy) caring for Jo, but also by role reversals between mother and daughter, during Act One especially. It is Jo who takes on the parental responsibility of trying to use the stove in the first scene, and she repeatedly fields questions from Helen, such as 'Where's my hat?' (61). This role reversal comes from Helen's dependency on Jo, and expectation that her daughter should look after her; it is partly resolved by Helen taking on motherly responsibilities in the final scene. Delaney highlights how the character in the parental role switches from Jo to Helen by showing Helen attempting to use the stove, and Jo repeating the advice that Helen gave her, almost word-for-word, when she was trying to do the same thing months earlier. This swopping of roles is undermined by Helen's last departure, which reinforces her inadequacy as a mother. With her exit, it is the daughter who is the closer of the two to parenthood – literally, in labour – when the play ends. The fact that the parent/child roles that Helen and Jo take on are incomplete and changeable underlines this is not a traditional relationship. It is therefore relevant to the portrayal of motherhood and maternal relationships, as well as the theme of families.

Other failures to fulfill family roles are linked to marriage. Along with Helen's first marriage (part of her backstory), neither Boy nor Peter's proposals result in happy marriages. As an extension of this, in his role as Jo's stepfather, Peter refuses her money and a room in his house; this goes against the sort of support expected of an 'ideal' father figure, especially in the 1950s.

The only successful 'marriage' in the play is that of Geof and Jo, which only ends because of an outside influence (Helen). Geof takes the position of a surrogate husband, emphasized by his accepting Jo's offer to be her baby's father. After Jo has refused his sexual advances, Geof expresses insecurity: 'I don't suppose I could live up to that black beast of a prince of yours' (91). This comparative mention of the absent father highlights that Geof is a replacement. However, it is the alternative household of Geof, Jo and the unborn child that creates the warmth and support expected of a model, traditional family. This is an unconventional 'family' because of Geof and Jo's sexless relationship, Geof's homosexuality and talent for 'wifely' duties that Jo lacks, and the fact that the baby will be mixed-race. This aspect of *Honey* presents a challenge to a society in which 'normal' (heterosexual) families were celebrated, and mixed-race families and homosexuality considered socially unacceptable.

Geof's proposal is the only one to be declined. Acting spontaneously, as both Jo and Helen do in accepting marriage offers, leads to unhappy circumstances. Romantic and sexual relationships, and what results from them, allow for a 'taste' of excitement, but not long-term happiness. Indeed, sex creates problems: Helen's decision to have an affair outside a sexless marriage caused her to become a divorced, single mother, just as Jo's relationship with Boy leads to her being unmarried and pregnant. Jo and Geof's 'marriage' works because it is platonic.

During Act One, Jo says to Helen, 'It's the darkness inside houses I don't like' (47). On the surface, this line is about being afraid of the dark. However, its importance lies in showing Jo's negative feelings about family life, associated with being 'inside' a home, which result from her upbringing. This fits with Jo's attitude towards being a mother and – despite her engagement – marriage.

Things to do

1 In groups, script and perform a one-minute television advert for a 1950s household product that features the 'perfect' 1950s family. Your audience should compare and contrast your characters with those in *Honey*.

2 Make a list of the things that Geof does which make him a good surrogate (mother, husband and father-to-be). Now, imagine you are Geof after he has left the flat, and decide to write to Helen to try to convince her that you should be allowed to move back in. Write Geof's letter to Helen, including some or all of the items on your list.

Hereditary characteristics

Something 'hereditary' is passed down from previous generations, like eye colour or height. If you were to say, 'I get this talent from my Dad', you would be describing a hereditary characteristic.

This theme is portrayed through Jo's worries about her, and her baby's, mental health, which come from what Helen tells her about her father. Geof's mention of *Ghosts* (1881), a famous drama by a Norwegian playwright called Henrik Ibsen, emphasizes Jo's concerns. This play is about a young man finding out he was born with syphilis, inherited from his father; in this form, the disease affects the brain. Jo's anxieties about sanity are shown through insecurity and depression. The 'darkness inside houses' that she fears does not just describe the difficulties of an unsettled family life, but hints that families are a source of depression: perhaps in a literal, hereditary sense. Imagery of darkness is often used to represent depression in our culture.

Cyclical behaviour

Something that is 'cyclical' happens in cycles; it describes things that repeat or are 'on a loop'. In *Honey*, it relates to action, and recurring patterns of behaviour.

While Jo frets over what she may have inherited from her father, her actions are a lot like her mother's. Jo's repeating of what Helen has done is key to this theme; it has the effect of making Jo's criticisms of her mother, and her claim to be unlike her, ironic.

Through important life events, Delaney shows Jo following in Helen's footsteps: sex, pregnancy, marriage and single parenthood. In addition, the closing scene reveals that Helen, like Jo, was neglected as a child. This hints that Helen has reproduced her own mother's behaviour. The theme also unfolds through more subtle facts and events: both Jo and Helen experience a first job in a pub, and an actual or surrogate sexless marriage; their key, unsuccessful relationships in the play are with men (Boy and Peter) associated with jobs in the military; Helen gives Jo her cold. As events in the calendar year are cyclical, the theme is emphasized by the fact that Jo gets pregnant at Christmas time, and Helen went into labour on Christmas Eve. A close link between cyclical behaviour and the theme of motherhood is underscored by this last example.

Similarities of personality and attitude are another way that Delaney shows Jo repeating Helen's behaviour. Apart from their shared resistance to 'ideal' motherhood, both women's impulsive streak is part of a generally disorganized manner. While this is more obvious in Helen's case, Jo's own habit of not planning ahead is shown not just through her relationship with Boy, but her drawings, which Geof describes as 'exactly like' her, because they have 'no design, rhythm or purpose' (79).

This theme is also dramatized through the characters as individuals: Helen, in particular. Much of her behaviour, like drinking, is habitual, and therefore cyclical; her relationship with Peter is a repetition (as they were together before), and their marriage is her second, and fails, like her first. Visually, Helen's final appearance with her belongings in the final scene echoes the very start of the play, just as Helen and Jo, alone together towards the end, mirrors the opening of Act One. This shows how the play's structure supports the cyclical theme, which you can read more about under 'Dramatic technique'. The idea that the characters represent people locked in a cycle of poverty is addressed in one of the extracts that feature in 'Critical reception and writings'.

Things to do

1 In groups, create two or three tableaux (freeze frames) that represent reasons why Jo dislikes the darkness 'inside houses'. You might include events and people from her past.

2 Create a timeline for Helen and Jo that includes things that they both do, using a different coloured pen/font for each of them. Make it clear which events are part of the characters' backstories, and which happen in the play itself.

3 Read the section of Act Two, Scene Two that begins with Jo saying, 'hold my hand', and ends with the stage direction *She pushes his hand away* (71–2).

(a) How does this extract show cyclical behaviour?

(b) How are Jo's actions ironic?

Write your answers to these questions in complete sentences, as if they were part of an essay.

Death and ageing

Death is a secondary theme. None of the characters in the play actually die, although Jo's father, a key *offstage* character, is dead.[9] Death imagery appears in the dialogue, especially during the first scene (for example, in Jo's dream about Helen being 'under a rosebush' [36]). It is also represented by the flat's

---

[9] An offstage character is part of the story, but does not ever appear on the stage. The children outside the flat are also offstage characters: they are only heard or talked about.

location near a slaughterhouse and cemetery, and through mentions of other drama in which it is important (*Ghosts* and Shakespeare's *Othello*). Helen's unsentimental attitude to death mirrors her approach to life: she accepts that life must end, just as periods of pleasure are only ever 'tastes'. This is appropriate to someone who lives 'in the moment'.

This theme reinforces Jo's description of life as 'chaotic – a bit of love, a bit of lust and there you are' (107). This line encapsulates the way that Delaney represents life through the female characters: driven by instincts and impulses, rather than thought and caution. Jo tells Helen that her relationship with Geof is sexless by saying 'we're so decent we're almost dead' (93). Geof's expressions of love for Jo includes the line, 'Before I met you [. . .] I didn't care whether I lived or died' (92). Death, in the play, is an absence of love or desire. It is fitting that death imagery appears in Jo's reactions to becoming a mother, including her view of breastfeeding as 'cannibalistic' (89).

Despite her attitude to death, the process of ageing troubles Helen, and it is through her that this related theme is presented. Peter's age (ten years her junior), and Jo's age and pregnancy, are important to this. The connection between the second two of these is shown by repetition of language. When Peter first sees Jo in Act One, he observes that she 'puts another ten years on' Helen (39); Helen later tells Geof, 'Oh, shut up, you put years on me' (94) in response to him pointing out that Jo's baby will be her grandchild. Both Jo and Peter emphasize Helen's age through comments about it. Associations between Jo and childhood reinforce the age gap between the women. These include Jo's collection of children's books, the titles of which Helen reads out ('*Selected Nursery Rhymes*, [. . .] *Pinocchio*' [62]). Other visual elements of the play reflect Jo and Boy's youthfulness, and are discussed in the 'Character' section. Finally, Helen's ageing fuels her resentment for Jo; it is Jo's actions, after all, that mean she is to become a grandmother. The link between this theme and the mother–daughter relationship is discussed by Lesley Sharp, who played Helen at the National Theatre in 2014, in a newspaper interview, available online at: http://www.theguardian.com/culture/2014/feb/08/lesley-sharp-interview-taste-of-honey.

Things to do

1 In pairs, find two lines from the first scene that show Helen's matter-of-fact attitude towards death.

2 Compare and contrast Peter's references to Helen's age in Act One with those in Act Two. Write down individual words that reflect how his feelings change.

Character

After reading any of the character analyses below, close this book and write down as many key characteristics as you can remember. Next, try to find your own evidence from the play for each characteristic you have listed. This could be something that is said (dialogue) or something that is done (action). Share your work with a pair or group to build up a bank of 'evidence', including quotations, about all of the characters.

The female characters

Jo

Jo is the play's protagonist: the action depicts her progress from schoolgirl to expectant mother, and she features in the play's two key relationships, with Helen and with Geof. Jo is a sympathetic character because she is neglected and abandoned by Helen and Boy. Although she claims to be 'Nearly eighteen' (48) in Act One, the fact that school leaving age was fifteen in 1958 suggest this is not true.

The play's title relates most obviously to this character, reinforcing her importance. Jo's 'taste of honey' (an idea introduced in 'Themes') is the short-lived relationship with Boy, for which she is 'punished' by pregnancy and a return to living with Helen. On one occasion, Boy calls her 'honey' (52) as a pet name. However, the relationship that Jo has with Geof is also a 'taste of honey': he too represents a break for Jo, from her mother, and offers a degree of support that Helen fails to provide. Care and affection motivate Jo to behave more warmly and openly with both Geof and Boy than she does otherwise; in Helen's company, she is often private and defensive.

As discussed under 'Themes', it is as a daughter *and* expectant mother that Jo upsets traditional ideas about maternal behaviour and relationships. The emotional distance created by calling her mother 'Helen' underlines her wish to put *actual* distance between them: expressed through her desire for a job, in Act One, and her refusal to to let Helen move back into the flat at the end of Act Two, Scene One. During her pregnancy, Jo demonstrates resistance to looking after anything other than herself, which is something else she has in common with Helen. Jo tells Geof that 'I always want to have you with me because I know you'll never ask anything from me' (113) during their final moments alone together. Her earlier claim that he is 'nothing' to her, and she is 'everything' to herself (90) is contradicted by evidence of thoughtfulness and generosity, such as accepting a cigarette from Helen in order to give it to him. However, a belief in putting oneself first, inherited from Helen, persists in Jo, shaping her approach towards motherhood. She remarks to Geoff of the baby that 'I might call it Number One. It'll always be number one to itself' (113). This suggests that she expects her child to inherit this attitude, and that it will no more be 'number one' to her than she has been to Helen.

At points, Jo is self-sufficient and demonstrates that she does not want to rely on anyone anymore than she wants anyone to rely on her. This is a result of Helen's neglectfulness.

By the start of Act Two, with Helen gone, Jo has taken responsibility for the rent on the flat and tells Geoff that 'I've got to work all day in a shoe shop and all night in a bar to pay for it. But it's mine. All mine' (77). The sense of pride suggested by the repetition of 'all mine' shows that independence is important to her, as does her refusal to accept Helen's support in the first half of Act Two. Moreover, Jo is not upset over the fact that her boyfriend does not return as promised, and tells Helen that it would be 'degrading' (117) to try to find him for financial support.

However, Jo's self-sufficiency is limited by insecurity and dependence on others. This side of her also stems from Helen's behaviour. Shortly after Helen has told Jo that she is going to marry Peter in Act One, Jo 'attacks' him, 'half-laughing, half-crying', and says: 'You leave me alone. And leave my mother alone too' (57–8). This moment demonstrates the bond between the women, and the fact that Jo does not like to be alone. Although Jo becomes more independent as the action progresses, she insists Geof move in in Act Two, Scene One. Furthermore, when Helen makes to go to the pub at the end of the play, Jo's heightened sense of dependency is shown through her questions: 'Are you just going for a drink?'; 'Are you coming back?' (125) and the fact that she recites one of the 'Geof's' nursery rhymes for comfort.

Jo's fear of the dark 'inside houses' is a further insecurity, and refers to the symbolic 'darkness' of unsatisfactory family life (see 'Themes' for more information). In addition, apparent confidence about her beauty and talent is presented as a mask for personal doubts. Threatened by Helen's attractiveness, she flirtatiously asks Peter, 'Do you fancy me?' (60) and questions Boy over whether he 'fancies' Helen and thinks she is 'beautiful' (66). When Boy replies 'Yes' to the second of these question, Jo's next line is, 'Am I like her?', to which he responds, 'No, you're not like her at all' (66). The idea that Jo does not look like her attractive mother suggests a reason for her physical insecurities, which are compounded by the suggestion that she may look like her father; Helen tells her that she has inherited his 'strange eyes' (74). Jo's father's role as a catalyst for her worries about psychological health is reinforced in this way: if she has inherited his looks, perhaps she has also inherited the mental deficiencies that Helen tells her about. It is worth noting, however, that these 'deficiencies' are never confirmed as facts, and Jo is not mentally ill, despite a tendency to feel depressed.

As Jo values self-preservation, and longs to be self-sufficient, yet is dependent on others and insecure, she is a complex character. One of the things that *does* not change about her is the tendency to be changeable, particularly during Act Two. In the same scene in which she throws the doll, she tells Helen that '[. . .] I feel as though I could take care of the whole world' (119). It is possible to see Jo's mood swings as a consequence of the hormonal changes that come with being both a teenager and pregnant, but she is also inconsistent in Act One, informing Helen that she will not marry in the first scene, and becoming engaged to Boy in the second. Her response to his proposal is 'I won't marry you but you've talked me into it' (48), a line which sums up her contradictory nature. Like the impulsive decision to invite Boy to stay, this shows another element of Jo's character that ties her to Helen: a strong spontaneous streak.

Finally, Jo is creative and imaginative. When Helen observes that she is 'always dreaming' (123) in the final scene, it is because Jo has just woken from a dream (the second of two she has). However, her line is a suitable description of Jo's habit of daydreaming and indulging in romantic fantasies, such as those about Boy (looked at further in the section about him). Although Jo is genuinely attracted to Boy, he is, primarily, a fantasy for her. She calmly predicts that he will not fulfil his promise to return, and is not heartbroken when this happens, describing him in the last scene as 'only a dream I had' (112). Jo also embellishes Helen's account of her father and the afternoon 'love affair that lasted five minutes' (73), telling Geof that she was conceived as the result of 'A frolic in a hay loft' (109). The way in which the play as a whole has a dreamlike quality is considered under 'Dramatic technique'.

Jo's drawings also indicate her romantic tendencies – Geof tells her they are 'sentimental' (79) – and represent the character's creativity. In a moment of rare praise, Helen describes her drawings as 'very good' (37) and even Geof, who is more critical, can see potential in her work. The duologues between mother and daughter further represent Jo's creativity and imagination; she is quick-witted and has a dry, rather dark sense of humour. Finally, the pregnancy is highlighted as a literally creative characteristic when Jo reflects, in Act Two, 'I'm certainly creating at the moment' (80).

Other aspects of this character, including her relationship with Helen, are explored under 'Themes.'

Helen

Helen is a central character because of her relationship with Jo. She became a single mother in her mid-twenties, having been divorced by her husband for a sexual encounter that left her pregnant. Her occupation of 'semi-whore' (29) is one of having boyfriends who provide her with enough money to live; however, she is not a prostitute. Her treatment of Jo and Geof make her largely unsympathetic. Relevant sections of 'Themes', and Sally Lindsay's reflections on playing the character ('Behind the Scenes'), can help you with understanding that Helen is not simply a 'bad' mother.

Helen's 'taste of honey' is her marriage to Peter, as this gives her an improved standard of living; the 'punishment' is being left for another woman, and returning to a life of financial struggle. The affair with Jo's father is also a 'taste of honey', despite not being part of the action.

Jo gets away from problems mentally, through fantasising; Helen's reaction is to *physically* re-locate. For example, she moves to the flat with Jo in order to try and 'escape' (39) from Peter. When mother and daughter are discussing being in labour, Helen answers the question, 'Did you yell?' with 'No, I ran' (123). This shows how she perceived Jo as a problem even before she was born. Moving house is a long-term habit of

Helen's, showing that she tries to flee difficult circumstances frequently.

As a source of escapism, alcohol is a second means by which Helen looks to distance herself from her problems. Comments of Jo's suggest that her mother is dependent upon alcohol, and drinks excessively, and Helen's actions match her claims. Helen's dependency upon drink is emphasized through its association with Peter and their relationship.

Helen's attitude to motherhood is a crucial aspect of the play, shaping her relationship with Jo, and Jo's own perspective on maternal responsibilities. Indeed, Helen's inadequacy as a mother is her most obvious feature. Like the habits of moving and drinking, her neglect of Jo is a long-standing characteristic.

Helen's ability to be maternal, despite a generally unmaternal manner, shows that she, like Jo, is contradictory. (You can read more about this idea in 'Themes'.) This aspect of the character is also created through her attitude to choice and destiny. In Act One, she tells Jo: 'There's two w's in your future. Work or want [. . .]. We're all at the steering wheel of our own destiny. Careering along like drunken drivers' (55–6). On the one hand, Helen thinks Jo can shape her future by choosing between being employed ('work') and going without ('want'), and the metaphor of driving a car represents being in charge of one's life. On the other hand, the reference to 'drunken drivers' suggests that Helen believes it is very difficult to control one's future, which is reinforced by the word 'destiny'. This contradiction is shown, too, through the way that Helen expects Jo to make choices based on the advice she gives her (such as not to get married), but also tells her 'don't think. It doesn't do you any good' (75). Ultimately, Helen is more fatalistic than not.

A disorganized, chaotic and impulsive character, Helen did not notice that the flat leaked before moving into it, nor that Jo's school is 'miles and miles' (35) away. These oversights support Jo's view that she does not think things through. Helen's disorganization is also represented through her not being able to find her possessions at various points. In Act Two, when Jo does not believe her mother's promise that she will remember to send money, Helen replies: 'I don't forget things; it's just that I can't remember anything' (98). This is an important quotation, highlighting that Helen is contradictory, thoughtless rather than spiteful, and – for her faults – very honest.

As an impulsive woman, Helen lives 'in the moment', accepting Peter's proposal, for instance, having moved once to escape him. Her desire for pleasure goes hand-in-hand with her habit of (literally) running away from responsibility and problems. A lack of forward-thinking is part of Helen's fatalism; she does not believe it is possible to improve her life long-term. Indeed, 'she will try various means of escape, but never with any great conviction that they will work, and when things go wrong [. . .], she is not really surprised' (Taylor 1963 [1962]: 114). Consequently, Helen is not heartbroken over Peter. This is similar to Jo's calm acceptance of Boy's disappearance. Living 'in the moment' means that both women accept it when pleasant experiences turn out to offer no more than a 'taste' of joy.

Her neglectfulness and impulsivity position Helen as a selfish character. The following duologue, in Act Two, demonstrates her honesty about this:

> **Jo**   [. . .] all those months you stayed away, just because of him! Just like when I was small.
> **Helen**   I never thought about you! It's a funny thing, I never have done when I've been happy. (118)

This quotation also reflects Helen's characteristic of putting men before Jo, first established in the opening scene during Peter's visit. On the other hand, Helen's relationships with men are her source of income, and therefore benefit Jo. Helen's decision to marry Peter – a wealthy man – reflects her strong instinct for survival and self-preservation. She often looks for ways to acquire money and possessions out of others. Indeed, her jokingly wondering if she can make a profit out of Jo by turning her into a film star highlights a habit of seeing people (usually men) as potential means of income. Through the monologue about her childhood towards the end of the play, Delaney hints that Helen was neglected in her youth. This gives a possible reason for Helen's ruthless approach to survival and is a sympathetic part of the character, especially because of parallels with Jo.

Helen has a strong sexual appetite. She is also portrayed as attractive: both Peter and Boy praise her looks, and Jo is made to feel insecure by them (discussed above). There is a traditional connection between youth and beauty in our culture that includes the idea that women become less good-looking as they age. The fact that Helen is forty, ten years older than Peter, and still sexually appealing to him (at least at first), emphasizes her attractiveness.

In common with Jo, Helen has a creative streak, shown through her (love of) singing, and colourful, poetic use of language. She is often articulate and humorously sarcastic. Moreover, Helen loves to perform and has a highly expressive, theatrical manner, frequently beginning sentences with the exclamation, 'Oh!' (31). This aspect of the character is explored further under 'Dramatic technique'.

In reading the play, you may find Helen homophobic and racist. Her attitude represents views that were very common in the 1950s, as set out under 'Contexts'; since this time, ideas about prejudice, and the groups of people subject to it, have changed greatly. Helen's aggression towards Geof illustrates her wish not to be replaced in Jo's life. Feeling threatened, her homophobic insults are primarily a strategy that she uses to intimidate him into moving out. This is the function of the homophobic language, and it is more important to understand this than to consider homophobia as a key part of Helen. At the very end of the play, Helen's shock highlights that a child of 'mixed race'– and mixed-raced relationships – were not socially acceptable in 1958. As single motherhood was also frowned upon, Jo's pregnancy and her baby make her a double target for society's disapproval. Helen's line, 'Can you see me wheeling a pram with a . . .' (125) reflects this, showing concern specifically with the opinions of others. Finally, Helen's (racial) prejudice is not a central aspect of the character because it only appears at the very end and is not established in the first scene, in which all of her principle features are shown. An audience watching the play would not be *able* to view Helen as racist for the majority of the performance. As a GCSE student, you will probably read this drama more than once. Helen's display of racism highlights the importance of considering a play from the point of view of someone seeing it in a theatre, for the first time.

The male characters

The male characters are secondary to the female. Geof is the most significant of the three, reflected in the fact that he, too, experiences a 'taste of honey' enjoying his time with Jo before Helen bullies him out of the flat. The other two men also enjoy a short period of living with one of the women, but they are not 'punished': Peter chooses to rejects Helen, and Boy's future remains unknown.

Geof

Geof is a gay art student in his late teens or early twenties. His importance in the play owes to his relationship with Jo, and – like Peter – the way he comes between the female characters. He highlights Helen's possessiveness of Jo, and her jealousy over someone else playing a maternal role in her daughter's life. Geof is a sympathetic character because of his selflessness, and the unpleasant way that Helen and Peter (and Jo, at points) treat him.

Jo's friendship with Geof unmasks aspects of the character that lie behind her defensive exterior. This stems from his nurturing, kind and gentle behaviour, but is also because their relationship is fun and playful. This is established in their first scene, when they return from a fairground and 'enter the flat playing about with a bunch of brightly coloured balloons' (76). Later, Jo openly fantasises that her boyfriend came 'From darkest Africa!' and was called 'Prince Ossini!' (85). Geof responds supportively to these fictitious claims. The pair recite nursery rhymes, and 'dance together' (104) at the close of Act Two, Scene One; the only couple in the play to do so. It is also with Geof that Jo sings for the first time. Earlier, in Act One, Helen throws doubts on her ability to do so: 'You can't sing, can you?' (36). Finally, Geof's warmth towards Jo reveals a generous side to her character. He allows her a degree of self-expression and openness rarely possible with Helen.

Geof is a 'closeted' gay character, meaning he hides his homosexuality: it is through Jo, Helen and Peter's comments that an audience learn he is gay. His sexuality is never confirmed, reflecting the laws surrounding homosexuality – in plays and in reality – in the 1950s (see 'Contexts').

The romantic advances that Geof makes stem from the wish to create a family unit with Jo, rather than indicating romantic desire. After refusing his proposal, Jo announces that she is going to lie down, and does so. This is later revealed as a way that Jo showed Geof she would have consented to a sexual relationship with him:

> **Geof** Do you remember when I asked you to marry me?
> [. . .] You just went and lay on the bed.
> **Jo** And you didn't go and follow me, did you?
> **Geof** No.
> **Jo** You see, it's not marrying love between us [. . .]. (112)

It is not just that Jo rejects Geof; Geof refuses Jo by not taking up her wordless invitation. Given his declarations of love for her, this reinforces Geof's homosexuality.

Geof's practical, emotional and financial support of Jo is central to his character, and the attention that she receives from him in the second act contrasts with Helen's neglect in the first. His 'maternal' skilfulness is underlined by his concern for the unborn child, and threatens Helen's position in Jo's life as a mother and future grandmother. As a surrogate, Geof proves a better parent than the play's only biological one. This strength, along with his ability to perform domestic jobs, associates Geof with traditional women's roles (as explored in 'Themes'). The play's language strengthens this connection, such as when Jo responds to Geof's statement, 'Motherhood is supposed to come natural to women' by saying 'It comes natural to you [. . .]. You'd make somebody a wonderful wife' (87). Similarly, Jo refers to Geof as 'big sister' (86), while Peter calls him 'Mary' (100) as a homophobic insult.

Peter

Peter is a thirty-year-old car salesman, and a former boyfriend of Helen's when the play begins. Through him, the audience learn that Helen's relationships with men are also a sort of job: he calls the flat her 'new headquarters' (39), for example. Peter is a barrier between Helen and Jo that makes Jo jealous, just as Geof frustrates Helen through his intimacy with Jo. Peter's insensitive behaviour makes him unsympathetic.

Peter tells Jo that he wears a black eye patch because he 'lost an eye' (59) in the war. The youngest age at which British men could go into combat was eighteen, and Peter would have been seventeen when World War Two ended (1945). Some teenagers did lie about their age in order to be able to fight, but Peter's story may not be true. He is an untrustworthy character: claiming that his interest in Helen is because he is not attracted to 'sweet young things' (60), then leaving her for a younger woman, for instance.

Peter is superficial. Despite the proposal, the interest he shows in Helen, in Act One, is sexual. Joking about the age gap between them at this early stage, he uses it as a means to insult her later on. In Act Two, Peter shows that he regrets his marriage by comparing himself to Oedipus – the protagonist of an Ancient Greek play called *Oedipus Rex* by Sophocles – who tears his eyes out when he realizes that his wife is also his mother.

Unlike Helen, Peter is wealthy. This is represented by his cigar, and the fact he shows off about his money through flashy, ostentatious behaviour, such as jokingly bragging to Jo that his big house has 'twelve swimming pools' (58). Peter is critical of Helen's flat and its unpleasant location. In Act Two, his views expand into a criticism of both female characters and Geof, all of whom he describes as having 'no class at all' (103).

Peter's snobbishness is hypocritical as his own behaviour lacks sophistication. Apart from his vulgar displays of wealth, he is insulting and malicious: to Helen about her age, Jo about her pregnancy, and Geof about his sexuality. Whether or not he really was a Private during the war, this part of the character adds irony to his manner of looking down on others: it is the lowest rank in the Army. A tendency to dominate the people he is with and space he is in adds to Peter's brashness. This is at its most extreme when he drunkenly crashes and shouts his way about the flat in Act Two. His heavy drinking, more generally, lowers the character's status. An audience might consider Peter ridiculous, especially because – while being threatening – he is not always fully in control of his actions (falling over in the second act, for instance). This is considered further under 'Dramatic technique'.

In terms of women, Peter is promiscuous. This is hinted at by the photographs of women that Jo spots in his wallet, and confirmed through his infidelity. He is even slightly flirtatious with Jo, saying 'Not yet' (60) when she asks if he fancies her. (This also shows that Peter is not an 'ideal' stepfather, about which there is more under 'Themes'.) Peter's attitude is one that an audience, today, might consider sexist. He lacks respect for Helen and Jo, and talks about other women as if they are (sexual) objects, describing the young woman with whom he had an affair as 'a couple of grapefruit on a thirty-two bust' (101). At the same time, Peter's promiscuity shows that he is seductive and has the ability to attract and charm others. These characteristics are also represented by his career as a successful salesman, and his ability to convince Helen to marry him, even though she had left him once before. The connection between his job and his personal life is captured by the 'sales speak' that he uses to propose, telling Helen that she 'won't find anything better' (43).

Boy

Boy is a twenty-two-year-old black sailor from Cardiff, and Jo's boyfriend. He is in the Navy to complete his National Service, which was compulsory for young men in Britain from 1948 to 1963. Through Boy, Delaney portrays attitudes to people from racial minorities, and interracial relationships. Jo's pregnancy means that these ideas extend beyond Boy's two scenes, into Act Two.

Boy features as a 'taste of honey' for Jo because he gives her affection and attention. This is playful and romantic as well as sexual, such as when he '[swings] her through the air' (49). Although her relationship with Geof is completely different, Jo's open, excitable manner with Boy is similar to how she behaves with him. Boy is sexually experienced and seductive; importantly, he shows an audience that Jo, like Helen, has a sexual appetite. Boy has a caring, nurturing side, in common with Geof. This is indicated by his former job as a nurse, and the way he looks after Jo after Helen and Peter leave in Act One. Boy's treatment of Jo is likely to make him sympathetic to an audience, but this perspective may change when he does not return. However, there is no indication that Boy knows about the pregnancy.

Despite being several years older than Jo, Boy is youthful and somewhat immature. The couple's light-hearted duologue, when they become engaged, does not suggest a serious approach to the future. Moreover, the superficiality of their relationship is shown through Boy's admittance that he 'couldn't remember' (49) the size or shape of Jo's hands. The characters are also associated with childhood through costume and props: Jo in her school uniform; Boy carrying schoolbooks;

both of them playing with his toy car. These visual elements reinforce the immature quality of their relationship, which is confirmed by the fact that their marriage plans come to nothing.

Crucially, Boy is a figure of fantasy for Jo, as has already been touched upon. By making 'Boy' his official character name, Delaney presents him as a sort of blank canvas onto which Jo can project her fantasies, much like a doll that a child can dress up as they choose. A feature of a fantasy is that it is usually private, and Jo is only ever seen alone with Boy. Another is that it can change. This is reflected in the different names connected with Boy, who compares himself with Shakespeare's Othello and is called 'Prince Ossini' (85), and (his real name of) Jimmie, by Jo.

The fantasies Jo invents with Geof about Boy echo an earlier duologue:

Jo   [. . .] Did your ancestors come from Africa?
Boy   No. Cardiff. Disappointed? [. . .]
Jo   I don't care where you were born. There's still a bit of jungle in you somewhere. (51)

Jo's words could seem racist to a contemporary audience. However, her ideas about Boy's ancestry are part of the fantasy she invents about him. He is a source of escapism when she can pretend that he does not come from a British city like her, but an utterly different place. As Boy is not an immigrant, this also makes the point, at a time of interracial tensions, that there were black communities in Britain long before the 1950s. Through imagination, Jo's ideas about Boy distance her from her dissatisfying life. The *actual* outcome of their relationship – her pregnancy – is something she cannot escape. It is only in the final scene that Jo tells Geof Boy is actually called Jimmie; he therefore keeps the status of fantasy figure for most of the play. This admittance shows that her daydreams are over, shortly before the reality of her future is signalled, undeniably, by labour.

Things to do

1 As a class, stage a prepared improvisation that puts Helen on trial for 'Crimes against Motherhood'. Some people should take individual roles (Helen; other characters as witnesses; a judge), and others should work in groups: prosecution lawyers, to argue that Helen is a 'bad' mother; defence lawyers, to argue that Helen has done her best; a jury to decide the verdict. If you are feeling confident about the play, volunteer to be one of the defence lawyers.

2 Create a series of tableaux (freeze frames) to represent the key features of any one of the characters: five or six for the women, and three or four for the men.

Dramatic technique

There are some references to television and cinema in this section. Both have been influenced by theatre, but are different forms of entertainment and representation. Re-read the guide to 'Reading a play' at the start of this book for a reminder of drama's unique features.

This section contains terminology that may well be new to you. One of the best ways to develop confidence in new terms is to practise using them in class discussions and writing tasks.

Key areas: form, structure and language

In the examination, you will analyse how form, structure and language contribute to the play's meanings and effects (explained further in 'Writing about the play'). Form refers to *how* a play is staged and performed as opposed to *what* it is about. Having an understanding of a play's form can help you to develop a more thorough appreciation of its structure and language. As you read this section, you will notice connections between all three of these areas. A summary has been provided at the end of the sections on form and structure.

Form

1. Kitchen sink realism

In 'Contexts', there is an introduction to kitchen sink drama: a category of playwriting that developed in the 1950s and represented 'everyday' experiences of working-class life, and related social issues, like poverty. The name comes from the fact that these dramas, including *Honey*, are set in domestic interiors (homes); they focus on personal relationships and struggles, often within families. Another name for kitchen sink drama is kitchen sink realism. 'Kitchen sink' refers to the particular themes being addressed; 'realism' describes the way in which these things are presented to an audience. For the most part, the form of the play is realism.

Realism first developed in the late nineteenth century and is associated with the Russian playwright Anton Chekhov, and Henrik Ibsen (who wrote *Ghosts*). In realism, 'real life' is represented on stage in an authentic style. This includes recognizable characters in recognizable situations, dialogue that sounds like real speech, and a stage set that accurately reflects the play's setting. For instance, the set of the 2014 National Theatre production actually looks like the interior of a rundown flat, as you can see from the images in the Background Pack. Realist characters have histories; like real people, they may have complex personalities. A good realist actor will make the audience connect with their character as if it were a real person, for example, by inducing feelings of sympathy for them.

Seeing a realist performance is like watching real people's lives unfold. These people (characters) are portrayed within a sealed-off 'world', as if in a bubble; they are separated from the reality of the theatre (the actual place where the performance takes place). In this case, the 'world' of the play is a flat in 1950s Salford. Although a drama may represent a real time and place, and real people (like historical figures), its world is a fictional one that the playwright has created. Importantly, to achieve the division between drama and reality, the actors pretend not to be aware of the audience.

2. 'Broken realism': dancing, singing and music

Some aspects of *Honey* are *non*-realist. This means that there is more to its form than realism, or, put another way, it is not 'pure' realism. Song, music and dance are not traditional elements of a realist play, yet the first two of these are used to portray believable situations and engage an audience with the characters (Jo singing in bed, secure in Geof's company, for example). On the other hand, these elements are also used to shatter this effect, or *interrupt* it; as a result, the play's form has been described as 'broken realism' (Aston 2008: ix).

Dancing that happens between scenes represents time passing. More traditionally, in drama, a lapse of time is represented by a blackout alone (described as 'fade out' [47] in the play). These moments are also non-realist because they are additions to the main action and narrative – not part of it – and jar with the atmosphere created by the characters' behaviour at points. For instance, after Helen '*dances on*' on her wedding day, suggesting a light-hearted mood, she snaps impatiently: 'Jo! [. . .] Be sharp now!' (68–9). Furthermore, the dancing does not portray differences between the individual characters. It creates a dream-like atmosphere that mirrors Jo's habit of daydreaming. This reinforces that she is the protagonist, and sympathetic; the audience are 'put in her shoes' by being given an unrealistic perspective of the world like the one she has in her fantasies.

Singing both adds to the realism and interrupts it. Like Jo's singing, Peter's bursts of song are realist, portraying his flirtation with Helen and brash personality. Contrastingly, both Boy and Helen's singing 'breaks' the realism. Boy, in his first scene, '*sings to the audience*' (53). Today, this sort of interaction might be associated with a concert or festival, rather than a play.

Helen's singing is non-realist because of its connection with the 'jazz trio' (27). Musicians appeared on stage in the first ever production, and have done so since, although recorded music is often now used as an alternative.[10] Helen's invitation to the musicians to play along to her singing disrupts realism because the people she is addressing are not characters in the play. Like Boy, Helen breaks the seal that separates the fictional 'world' of the stage from the *real* world of the theatre where the play is being performed.

'Broken' realism also occurs through the play's dialogue. Helen criticizes Jo through talking about her in the third person during the first scene. In various productions of the play – including the first – these comments were addressed directly to the audience. Their frustrated tone is echoed in one of Helen's very last lines: 'I ask you, what would you do?', which the stage direction indicates is said *'To the audience'* (125). In these cases, realism is interrupted by a technique called direct address, which involves an actor talking to an audience directly, usually with eye contact. However, Helen's third-person lines do not *have* to be performed in this way. In 'Behind the Scenes', director Bijan Sheibani explains that, for his production, it was decided Helen should be talking to herself. Performing the script like this means that realism is emphasized, not broken: the fictional 'world' remains intact. This example highlights the importance of interpretation to drama. Directors' and actors' approaches can shape dramatic form.

3. Music hall

Non-realist use of song, dance and music reflect the influence of a traditional form of British performance called music hall: a type of variety show that featured a range of acts such as

---

[10] A trio of musicians featured visibly in the 2014 Hull Truck production, as you can see several seconds into a promotional video, available online at: https://www.youtube.com/watch?v=OfYwH1NHQ6k.

singers and comedians. This was popular in the Victorian period, especially among working-class audiences, and an affordable source of fun entertainment. Music hall performers would directly address their audiences, as people today might be able to imagine from television variety shows like *Britain's Got Talent* (ITV, 2007–).

Music hall had become old-fashioned by the 1950s, and many of the songs in *Honey* were already classics by the time it was produced. For instance, Jo's 'Black Boy' (84) is a re-working of a folk song called *Where Did You Sleep Last Night?*, made famous in the 1940s. The original opening of this was: 'Black girl, black girl, don't lie to me.' Many of Peter's song snippets are 1920s classics. *Walter, Walter (Lead Me to the Altar)*, a 1928 track sung by Gracie Fields, 'mocks [. . .] popular ideals of love and marriage' (Szreter and Fisher 2010: 192). This reinforces the play's negative portrayal of romantic relationships. Music hall is also relevant to comedy, and the play's structure, which are discussed below.

4. 'Magnified realism': comedy and melodrama

Despite the play's serious themes, comedy stems from its dialogue and action. In many of their duologues, Jo and Helen exchange quick-fire criticisms and insults to try and outdo one another. They are sparring partners: a term which originally described boxers in training, but now means two people in an ongoing conflict. There is a pattern to their banter, and each of the women has a particular role to play: Helen's is to make elaborate claims, often in a theatrical way, and Jo's is to undermine them through dry, cutting responses. For example:

Helen   [. . .] My figure hasn't altered since I was eighteen.
Jo   Really?
Helen   Not an inch.
Jo   I hope I'm luckier with mine. (57)

These two *types* of character, together, form a pairing in comedy traditions that is associated with music hall. Peter and

Helen are another comedic duo, especially because of his repeated attempts to seduce her in Act One.

The chaotic atmosphere of Act Two, Scene One is created by Jo and Helen's argument, and Peter's drunkenness. The first of these is comedic because of the women's dramatic behaviour – the chase, Helen promising to kill Jo, Jo threatening to jump out of the window – which ultimately comes to nothing, as well as the presence of an innocent third character (Geof). By trying to defuse the situation, he becomes the target of both Jo and Helen's anger, and only cries out 'Will you stop shouting' (97) when there is a moment of silence. Sudden changes in the characters' allegiances echo the way that Helen jumps back and forth from Jo's defence to Peter's during Act One, and become even more complicated in this later scene when Peter enters, drunk. His crashing about and falling over (on- and offstage), like the women's 'chase', are slapstick in style. Slapstick comedy is highly physical; actions are exaggerated, ridiculous, and often seem to cause physical injury to the person performing them. Famously associated with silent film actor Charlie Chaplin, the award-winning live production, *The Play That Goes Wrong* (Mischief Theatre Company, 2012), is a famous recent example of slapstick. The loss of control and status that comes with this creates humour: an audience could well laugh at Peter in Act Two.

The heightened emotions that lead to slapstick in Act Two, and Helen's theatrical behaviour and speech, are melodramatic. Melodrama is an old-fashioned style of acting in which extreme emotions, like love and hate, are represented by exaggerated gestures. Its link to Helen is highlighted when she refers to Jo's situation, in Act Two, as a 'little Victorian melodrama' (94).

The melodramatic and slapstick elements have an effect on the play's form. These do not 'break' realism, but, instead, portray an exaggerated version of reality. If the realist elements work like a normal mirror (of society), these heightened styles of performance are like a hall of mirrors at a fairground, humorously caricaturing the things they reflect. A famous description of the play's premiere said it was 'a sort of *magnified realism* in which everything is like life but somehow larger than life' (Taylor 1963 [1962]: 113, my emphasis).

Form: summary

The play's main form is kitchen sink realism: a post-war type of realism. It also contains various styles of performance including dance and song, which show the influence of music hall. These have the effect of 'breaking' realism at points, and being part of it at others. Through direct address, dialogue can interrupt the realist effect. Comedy, melodrama and slapstick are further influences. These do not 'break' realism, but heighten or 'magnify' it. A director may choose to emphasize or play down one of more of these styles.

Things to do

In a small group, create a presentation for your class to show how you would direct a key scene of *Honey* to emphasize either (a) kitchen sink realism, (b) 'broken realism' or (c) 'magnified realism'. You may wish to find out more about influences on the play's form (such as slapstick) as part of your preparation. Include some acting to demonstrate your ideas.

Structure

1. Overview

The events of the play take place over nearly ten months: Act One is set in December 1958, and Act Two spans June to September of 1959. Both acts are made up of two scenes each, and every scene is split into sub-scenes by the passing of time, the entrance/exit of a character, or both.

2. 'Cause and effect'

The play's action unfolds chronologically, and all key events develop out of those that happen earlier. Many past and present events are catalysts: 'past' meaning set before the play begins, as opposed to the 'present' of the play itself. Therefore, the plot unfolds through 'cause and effect'. For instance, Peter's proposal causes Helen to abandon Jo. The effect of this is Jo asking Boy to stay with her, which causes her to become pregnant. This is a traditional approach to structure that stems from the Ancient Greek philosopher, Aristotle. Among the 'rules' for drama he developed was something called the 'unity of action', meaning that all events in a play should link to one another, in a chain of cause-and-effect, to create one story with no subplots. *Honey* does not fit this description exactly, but the importance of catalytic action shows Aristotle's influence.

3. Episodic features

The term 'episodic' means something that is divided into episodes. It will be explained further shortly.

Song, dance and music break up the action of *Honey* as it would unfold, over time, during a live performance. This is true even when these elements do not 'break' the play's realism. For instance, Jo's singing in front of Geof and their reciting of nursery rhymes are part of the main, realist action, showing intimacy between the two, yet stand out for being different in style from the pair's duologues. This contrast is highlighted by Jo describing her performance of 'Jack Spratt' as a 'dramatic recitation' (82).

Therefore, changes in styles of performance have an effect on structure as well as form. Although the play is mainly linear – one 'straight line' of connected action – the songs and so forth, by contrast, create an *episodic* effect by being different. This means that there are independent 'episodes' within the play, marking out sections within scenes as *separate* from one another. These divisions could be emphasized in performance by an audience's reaction, for instance if they were to clap after

Boy's song. As music hall is episodic through being made up of several separate performances, its influence can be seen in the play's structure, too.

4. The ending

In realist drama, television or film, what happens as the action unfolds, and the ending itself, are important. This is reflected in the term 'spoiler', to mean facts about forthcoming events (usually in a television drama), and expressions you may have heard, like 'don't tell me how it ends!'.

Some traditional, realist plays build towards an intense dramatic climax. This is followed by a final scene called a dénouement (French for 'conclusion'), which is usually calmer, and in which any 'loose ends' are explained or resolved, if not always happily. The audience feels that they have seen a complete, finished story. There is no one dramatic climax in *Honey*, despite tensions between characters reaching a peak in the first half of Act Two. The close is not a dénouement, but open-ended. Therefore, rather than offering a final conclusion, it is ambiguous about the characters' futures. This is reinforced by the last of the play's dialogue, much of which takes the form of questions. Helen's line of direct address, in particular, is an unanswered question that invites the audience to reflect upon the situation.

5. The cyclical theme

As a whole, the structure contains repetition and has a cyclical quality (introduced under 'Themes'). Both acts include scenes between Helen and Jo, interspersed with scenes between Jo and a male character to whom she is close (Boy or Geof). Parallels between the first and last scene emphasize how Jo and Helen represent cyclical patterns of behaviour: each has tried and failed to move on from their life together. There are repetitions, too, in the structure of some individual sub-scenes, underlining Jo and Helen's similarities. The first encounter between Jo and Boy echoes that of Helen and Peter. Both begin with the male character initiating a flirtation, and feature a marriage proposal delivered light-heartedly.

Structure: summary

There are two scenes in each of the two acts, each of which are divided into sub-scenes. Events unfold chronologically with lapses of time between, and within some, scenes. Song, dance, music and verse create an episodic effect, but the structure is still linear, because of the 'cause and effect' chain of events. It also has cyclical elements, and an open-ended close.

Things to do

In small groups, rehearse and perform a 'speed run' of the play. For each scene, come onto the 'stage' for a few seconds and say one key line/word per character. Discuss the following after watching each other's performances: how does the play's structure emphasize (a) Helen's characteristics as a mother, and (b) the difference between Jo's experiences with Helen, and with Boy or Geof?

Language

Two aspects of language have already been looked at: its role in 'breaking' realism through the way certain lines might be performed (form), and the role of questions in the last scene (structure). Delaney makes *some* use of regional dialect, which means ways of speaking in a particular part of a country. The opening word of Helen's line, 'Eee, there's a terrible draught' (34), for example, is a northern expression. Because it reflects how real people speak, dialect is a realist part of the language. The same is true of other colloquialisms, including dropped letters at the start of words, and lines of dialogue that are not grammatically accurate: 'It comes *natural* to you' (87, my emphasis). Realism also occurs through 'everyday' patterns of speech: unfinished or interrupted lines (shown by ellipses, which are '. . .', or dashes), sudden changes of subject, and duologues made up of questions and answers.

Language is relevant to historical context. The word 'coloured' (47) is used to describe Boy in the stage directions; this was a common, acceptable term in the 1950s for black and Asian people. One-word profanities (swear words) like 'slut' (103) appear as insults. These would have been considered more vulgar and explicit in the 1950s than they are today (except, perhaps, for the homophobic slang). When *Honey* was first staged, 'a member of the public wrote to the Lord Chamberlain [who was responsible for letting plays be performed] complaining about the "appalling use of blasphemy in the dialogue"' (Harding 2014: 46). This refers to the use of the word 'God' in expressing annoyance, which Helen does repeatedly. The profanities are another realist feature. The realism of the language, in general, supports Delaney's claim that 'I write as people talk' (Delaney in Kitchin 1960: 177).

Helen's mention of cinema listings also links dialogue to context. The films she names are from the same period as the play; *Desire Under the Elms* – the last word of which is not spoken – was released in March 1958, two months before *Honey* premiered.

Apart from the street outside the flat that forms part of the set, Delaney portrays the exterior (outdoor) location through language. This means the audience can picture the geographical setting. Some of the places mentioned are real; for instance, the river is the Irwell, which divides Salford from Manchester. Descriptive language is used to evoke the sights and smells of the city: 'dirty' washing on lines; 'filthy' children (86); a slaughterhouse that will stink in the summer.

Language reinforces the poor, urban context represented visually on the stage. The sounds an audience would hear, such as the *'hoots'* of a *'tugboat'* (86) and the voices and singing of children, are also important in representing Helen and Jo's Salford.

As in most realist drama, language is important to the portrayal of character. The quick-wit and humour of both female characters is presented through their duologues, as explored in terms of comedy. Helen's sarcasm is established in the first scene when she tells Jo, 'You know I can't bear to be parted from you' (30). Dialogue, too, shows Helen is articulate and intelligent; she tells Peter: 'The only consolation I can find in your immediate presence is your ultimate absence' (41). Her loud, theatrical personality is reinforced by flamboyant use of language; frequent exclamation marks suggest it should be performed in an equally flamboyant style.

Contradictions between what characters say and do hint that 'actions speak louder than words'. A marriage proposal is a verbal commitment that Peter and Boy both break. Jo's triumphant claim to be 'very unusual' (81) is undermined by her similarities with Helen, just as Helen's Act Two line, 'I love babies' (117), is one an audience might find infuriating or funny. Unlike the other two men, Geof does not praise and flatter, but speaks to Jo with unsentimental directness. His 'tough love' is matched by selfless behaviour; promises of love and support, made by other characters, are rarely followed through by action.

The poetic quality of some of Helen's speech furthers her expressiveness, such as when she uses the simile of a 'horizontal chimney' (41) to describe Peter's cigar. However, imagery is a feature of the language more broadly. Jo tells Peter that 'the art work takes a long time' (61) when Helen is preparing to go out; this is echoed by Peter's description of her, in the second act, as an 'unrestored oil painting' (99). This style is less close to how 'people actually talk'. As a heightened sort of expression, poetic imagery adds to the play's 'magnified realism'.

Things to do

Record a normal conversation between you and a friend. Listen to it and transcribe (write down) a short section of it as if it were a script, using correct punctuation (such as a dash to indicate an interruption). In your pairs, discuss similarities between your dialogue and the play's. Do you agree that Delaney writes how 'people actually talk'?

Set

The play's set is made up of the flat, and the street outside it. Domestic interiors (the inside of houses) are often connected with women, which fits the traditional view of a woman's 'place' being in the home. However, this connection is challenged, which is a feminist aspect of the play. The central part of the set is made up of the flat's bed, which is often centre-stage, as well as the living area (sofa). The room most strongly connected with women traditionally – the kitchen – is to one side. In the 2008 Royal Exchange production, it was offstage (meaning there was no 'actual' kitchen for the audience to see), and, in the National Theatre's 2014 version, the kitchen was not visible from every seat in the theatre. In a play about two women, therefore, the specific arrangement of this set represents a pushing aside of tradition. Although both Jo and Helen go into the kitchen, they are distanced from it, as most of the action takes place elsewhere. Delaney symbolically separates women from conventional ideas about their roles. The set also allows a glimpse of the exterior world through the street. The flat's windows are something a theatre designer might make use of to portray the city beyond. You can explore set design possibilities further through completing the activity below.

Costume and props

The costumes in *Honey* reflect the characters' roles and positions in society. As a schoolgirl, Jo wears a school uniform; as a mother-to-be, she wears a 'housecoat' (105), which is like a dressing gown, and was popular among 1950s housewives. Boy's profession is often represented by a conventional sailor's uniform. Helen's description of Jo's clothes as being 'held together by a safety pin or a knot' (63) indicates their lack of money, and poverty is reinforced by contrasts with wealth, through props as well as costume: Helen appears with 'fancy boxes' to greet Jo who is, 'in [. . .] pyjamas' (68–9) during Act One. Similarly, although the audience does not see the pink cot Helen tells Jo she has ordered for the baby, the mental image of it differs starkly from Geof's plain wicker basket.

Props are often symbolic, as considered in relation to food and drink under 'Themes'. For instance, Jo's hidden engagement ring signifies the lack of intimacy between her and Helen. (Jo literally keeps the symbol of her secret close to her chest. This is normally a figurative expression to mean being private about something.) In the 'Themes' and 'Character' sections, reference is made to props connected with childhood, like Boy's toy car. Props to do with babies further this theme in Act Two (as does the sight of Jo's pregnant body), and are reinforced by the sounds of children and spoken references to them. Together, the visual and aural representations of childhood emphasize the themes of motherhood and maternal relationships, but also youth: Jo's young age and Helen's childish behaviour.

Things to do

Design a set that is inspired by the characters' descriptions of the flat and the city beyond. Remember that the set is not just the flat, but the street, too. You may wish to draw ideas from online images and footage of past productions.

Critical reception and writings

'Reception', in this context, refers to how a play is received, especially by theatre critics and academics. This section is split into two parts. The first looks at journalistic reactions to the play from 1958. The second part contains short extracts from academic analyses of *Honey*.

Newspaper reviews

Today, the internet has made it possible for anyone with access to a computer to share their opinion about a play they have seen: for example, through blogging. This was not the case in the 1950s, 'a time when newspapers enjoyed large circulations, [and] theatre critics were important trend-setters and taste definers' (Pattie 2012: 41). What a critic wrote about a play, therefore, could have a huge impact on its success and popularity. *Honey* received mixed reviews when it was first staged, meaning that there were contrasting opinions about its worth and value. Edward Goring and Milton Shulman were two critics who were very critical in their reviews. These appeared in newspapers the day after the premiere.

Milton Shulman, Evening Standard, *28 May 1958*
The title of this review was 'A good try, Miss Delaney, but I couldn't believe it.' Shulman wrote that Delaney 'knows as much about adult behaviour as she does about elephants' and listed the names of famous male playwrights, from the late nineteenth century onward, whose work he suggested she should read. These included Henrik Ibsen and Tennessee Williams. The play itself, he described as being 'about as convincing as some dream fantasy watched through a distorting mirror'.

Edward Goring, Daily Mail, *28 May 1958*
Goring's asserted that the play '[tasted] of exercise books'. He wrote:

Once, authors wrote good plays set in drawing-rooms. Now, under the Welfare State, they write bad plays set in garrets.[11] [. . .] It hardly amounts to a play, and for all the shouting it says very little. It has a few touching moments, but those stem from the touching quality sometimes found in immaturity [. . .]. If there is anything worse than an Angry Young Man, it's an Angry Young Woman.

Negative reception

1   Both reviewers focus on Delaney as well as the play. Write down words to describe their tone, and attitude towards her.

2   What facts about Delaney are highlighted by these reviews? Consider the following language: 'exercise books'; 'adult behaviour'; 'immaturity; 'nice try'.

3   Schulman's review shows that he thinks Delaney needs to read work by famous playwrights. In pairs, imagine you have been asked to challenge him on this idea, using *Honey* as evidence. What would you say?

4   In the programme notes for the premiere, director Joan Littlewood described Delaney as 'the antithesis [opposite] of London's "Angry Young Men". She knows what she is angry about.' Improvise or script a duologue between Goring and a friend that takes place just after they have seen the play. The person playing Goring should explain why he considers an Angry Young Woman 'worse' than an Angry Young Man, and show understanding of historical context; the 'friend' should share Littlewood's opinion, and make references to the play.

5   Discuss the particular ways in which Delaney's writing is criticized. What do you recognize in Schulman's

---

[11] A garret is an attic room. This is a reference to *Look Back In Anger* (discussed in 'Contexts').

> writing from the 'Dramatic techniques' section of this
> book ('Form')?

The opinions of theatre critic Kenneth Tynan and novelist
Colin MacInnes contrasted with these views: they liked and
defended the play. Both use language that is now out-dated,
but would have been acceptable in the fifties. Look up any
words that are unfamiliar to you.

Kenneth Tynan, *Observer*, 1 June 1958

Miss Delaney brings real people on to her stage, joking and
flaring and scuffling and eventually, out of the zest for life
she gives them, surviving. [. . .] If I tell you that the heroine
was born of a haystack encounter between her mother and
a mental defective; that a Negro sailor gets her pregnant
and deserts her; and that she sets up house, when her mother
marries a drunk, with a homosexual art student [. . .], you
may legitimately suspect that a tearful inferno of a play
awaits you [. . .]. Not a bit of it.

The first half is broad comedy [. . .] and Joan Littlewood's
direction tilts it over into farce by making Avis Bunnage, as
the girl's brassy mother, address herself directly to the
audience, music-hall fashion.

[. . .] There are plenty of crudities in Miss Delaney's play:
there is also, more importantly, the smell of living. When the
theatre presents poor people as good, we call it 'sentimental'.
When it presents them as wicked, we sniff and cry 'squalid'.

Happily, Miss Delaney does not yet know about us and
our squeamishness [. . .]. She is too busy recording the wonder
of life as she lives it. There is plenty of time for her to worry
over [. . .] 'form' [. . .]. She is 19 years old: and a portent.

Colin MacInnes, *Encounter* magazine, April 1959

[The article was called 'A Taste of Reality'.]

Shelagh Delaney's *A Taste of Honey* is the first English
play I've seen in which a coloured man, and a queer boy,

are presented as natural characters, factually, without a nudge or a shudder. It is also the first play I can remember about working-class people that entirely escapes being a 'working-class play': no patronage, no dogma, just the thing as it is, taken straight. In general hilarious [   ], it gives a final overwhelming impressive [. . .] of a feeling for life that is positive [. . .].

[. . .]

It is, of course, wonderful that a woman of nineteen has written this play, but [. . .] no note of condescension is permissible on account of Shelagh Delaney's age. The play lives in its own right entirely.

[. . .]

The play gives great thirst for more authentic portraits of the mid twentieth-century English world. [. . .] Consider only some themes suggested in *A Taste of Honey*: what have we learned, elsewhere, about working-class child-mothers, ageing semi-professional whores, the authentic agonies of homosexual love, and the new race of English-born, coloured boys? [. . .] The last decade will be remembered as the one in which the biggest social changes happened and the very least was discovered about them by 'the arts'.

Positive reception

1   Tynan and MacInnes express very similar reasons for liking the play in the opening of these extracts. Discuss what these are in pairs.

2   Why can Tynan's review be seen as an attack on negative ones (through the last paragraph especially)?

3   As a class, discuss the following: in what ways does MacInnes consider *Honey* new and different? What is his opinion about 'the arts' in this period generally?

4   Compare and contrast these writers' attitude to Delaney with those of the negative reviews. (You may

want to think about what MacInnes means by 'The play lives in its own right entirely.') Are there any similarities as well as differences?

Academic responses

What follows are extracts from analyses of *Honey* by two different scholars. Their perspectives are designed to deepen your understanding of the play, and may challenge your views. The questions can be discussed in groups/as a class, used for writing tasks, or both.

Michelene Wandor

Wandor argues that, in the end, the mother–daughter relationship between Helen and Jo is stronger than the play's less conventional or socially acceptable relationships.

Wandor quotes Jo's line from Act Two, Scene Two: 'For the first time in my life I feel really important. I feel as though I could take care of the whole world' (119), then goes on to say: 'Motherhood feels possible [for Jo] when her own mother is there [. . .]. [The] mother/daughter relationship, however fraught, overrides any other kind of relationship' (Wandor 1987: 42). In an updated version of her analysis, Wandor argues: 'although all kinds of socially unconventional bondings look possible, in the end the biological [. . .] triumphs: the mother and daughter relationship overrides all taboos' (Wandor 2001: 62).

Questions
1   Apart from the quoted line in the first of these two extracts, can you find any other evidence for Wandor's view that Jo can face the thought of becoming a mother only when she is with Helen? Do you agree with the implication that motherhood does not 'feel possible' for Jo when she is with Geof?

2   What does Wandor mean by 'socially unconventional bondings'?

3   In 'Contexts', ways in which the play was radical and ahead of its time are discussed. Do you think the 'triumph' (or victory) of the biological relationship make the play any less radical? Could this 'triumph' have influenced the views of the censors who allowed it to be performed?

Edward J. Esche

Because of *Honey*'s themes, and the outcome for Jo, Esche challenges the idea that it is really a comedy. In this extract, he focuses on Jo at the end of the play and argues that comedic elements are a problem because they mask the serious social problems that the play portrays.

> As she screams in the pain of labour [. . .], the cycle of single mother trapped in poverty [. . .] may be starting all over again for the child about to be born. [. . .] [T]he jokes simply serve the function of papering over or disguising a pattern of social fracture [. . .]. There is resilience and humour throughout, but there is no solution offered to the cycle of decay.
>
> Esche 1994 [1992]: 78

Questions
1   Do you agree that the play's comedic elements 'paper over', or distract an audience, from the seriousness of the themes highlighted at the end of the play? You may wish to look at Sally Lindsay's account of different audience reactions to the final few minutes in performance ('Behind the Scenes'), and consider this question in relation to both a 1950s audience and one today.

2   Do you think comedy can be used to *highlight* serious themes in a play, novel or film? See if you can think of

any examples of this from other texts you have studied for GCSE.

3 Have you made an assumption about the sex of Jo's baby? If you were to write a sequel, would it be a girl or a boy, and why?

Related work

Look Back in Anger (1956) by John Osborne

As detailed in 'Contexts', this play marked the start of the British 'New Wave' of theatre. Like *Honey*, it is set in an unglamorous flat, and explores the themes of troubled families and unconventional households. Jimmy and Alison, unhappily married, share their home with friend Cliff, who shows Alison more affection than Jimmy does. Alison experiences a pregnancy and miscarriage; Jimmy is not sympathetic. The 'family' unit, seen on stage, changes: Alison leaves Jimmy and he begins an affair with her friend, Helena, who moves in; Cliff moves out in the final act. The core relationship between Jimmy and Alison is re-established in the last scene, as with Jo and Helen.

In *Honey*, the male characters function to reveal things about the female ones (such as their possessiveness of one another). Here, all the action revolves around Jimmy, a male protagonist with a sexist, hostile attitude to women.

The action of *Anger* takes place over several months, presented chronologically, with different lapses of time between the play's five scenes (contained within three acts). It has cyclical elements. The fact that Helena temporarily replaces Alison as Jimmy's partner is emphasized by her doing what Alison does at the start: wearing his shirt and ironing. Both dramas feature live singing and jazz, although alternative styles of music are sometimes used in productions of *Honey*. Jimmy talks about his love of jazz and plays it on the trumpet. This feature of the two plays reflects their shared historical context. Moreover, it is appropriate to the New Wave of theatre that jazz music 'signified [. . .] rebellion' (Harding 2014: 56) at this time.

The Lion In Love (1960) by Shelagh Delaney

This, Delaney's second play, was far less successful than *Honey*. A three-act drama, it is also set in an industrial, northern city and focuses on working-class characters. Kit and Frank are a married, middle-aged couple. She is an alcoholic, and irresponsible mother; he makes plans to run away with his lover, Nora, but does see them through. Younger and older generations are represented, in part through Kit and Frank's (grown-up) children, and Kit's ageing father. The drama extends beyond the family to portray other members of the community, including market traders. Various scenes take place outside, as well as within, the family home. The play has no protagonist. You can watch Delaney talking about the themes of *The Lion in Love* in *Shelagh Delaney's Salford*. This short film (available online at https://www.youtube.com/watch?v=iXmMsOBrx9g) also contains footage of the Salford markets that the play evokes.

A Taste of Honey (film, 1961) directed by Tony Richardson

Part of the reason for including this film is to highlight that it is *not* the same thing as the play you are studying, and should not be confused with it. A film version of a play exists as something completely separate from the play itself.

The film's screenplay (script) was co-written by Shelagh Delaney and the director, Tony Richardson, who also directed the play and film of *Look Back in Anger* (1956 and 1959). Shot in black-and-white in Greater Manchester and other parts of northern England, *Honey* was part of the British New Wave of cinema of the 1950s and 1960s, that – like the New Wave of theatre – represented working-class experience authentically.

This contrasted with glamorous Hollywood films. The film of *Honey* contains characters additional to those in the play, like Jo's schoolteacher, and several exterior (outdoor) scenes. Images of the film (stills) are available online.

My Mother Said I Never Should *(1987) by Charlotte Keatley*

As the title suggests, motherhood is a central theme of this female-authored play. Different generations of a family are represented through the play's four characters: Doris; her daughter, Margaret; her daughter, Jackie, and her daughter, Rosie. *My Mother Said* explores contrasting experiences of British women from various periods of the twentieth century. These contrasts are emphasized by the structure, as many of the scenes are in non-chronological order. This means that the audience are transported backwards and forwards in time over the course of the play, encountering the characters and their relationships with one another at various points in their lives. (Male characters, such as husbands, remain offstage.) The action, here, is realist, mirroring the experiences of real women in specific historical contexts.

These scenes are interspersed with non-realist ones, deliberately not set at any particular point in history, in which the characters appear as their childhood selves in a wasteground. In this context, the themes of mother–daughter relationships, sex, death and marriage are explored through children's games. In terms of the play as a whole, the women resent or struggle to conform to society's expectations of them as wives, daughters and mothers.

The Rise and Fall of Little Voice *(1992) by Jim Cartwright*

Set in the north of England, most of the action of this play unfolds in the dirty, disorganized home of Mari, a working-class, middle-aged widow, and LV (Little Voice), her shy teenage daughter who takes comfort in singing along to her late father's records. She has an incredible ability to mimic the voices of classic singers, like Marilyn Monroe. Mari is irresponsible, melodramatic and a heavy drinker; LV is resentful of her mother's poor parenting. Ray Say, who recruits acts to perform at a local club, becomes Mari's boyfriend. She is particularly interested in his wealth, having little money of her own. His real interest, however, is in making money out of LV's singing through employing her to sing at the club.

Certain scenes take place in the club, which is suggested to be like a town or school hall with a stage at one end. In performance, this often involves the actual theatre stage becoming the club stage, and the audience 'becoming' people at the club: the actor playing Ray directly addresses the play's audience to introduce LV as a new 'act', and the actor playing LV sings to them, as if at a concert. This aspect of the play interrupts the generally realist style by making the audience part of the action, echoing *Honey*'s form of 'broken realism'. Along with Mari's theatrical manner, the club scenes also suggest the influence of music hall on this play.

Glossary of dramatic terms

One of the things you will need to demonstrate in the examination is the ability to use a range of vocabulary to express your ideas in a focused and effective way. This, of course, will include subject-specific terminology. Keep in mind that terminology does not only consist of the more challenging words you will come across, and that you will know some key terms already. Take every opportunity to use terminology where relevant and appropriate. At points, this will simply mean replacing a word you would normally use for one better suited to drama: 'monologue' rather than 'speech', for instance. Including words without being careful because you think they sound impressive could lessen the quality of your essay. Use what you need, accurately, in order to answer the question.

Act   a major sub-section of a play, like the chapter of a book. An act might contain within it one scene or more, as in *Honey*. The events of an individual act can often be summarized as if it were a separate story (or narrative), independent of the rest of the text. The narrative of every act contributes to the narrative of the whole play. This can be compared to a football match, especially as the drama you are studying is in two acts! At the end of a match, a fan or commentator will often review what happened in each half separately, as a means to reflect upon the 'story' of the match as a whole. If you read theatre reviews, you will notice that it is common for journalists to make a comment about one act of a play in particular, or to draw comparisons between the quality of different acts. Referring to acts (and scenes) in essays can be a very effective way of orientating your reader: that is, explaining to them which particular part of the play you are looking at.

Action   things that characters do over the course of a play, usually driven by some sort of motivation. Motivation refers to something a character wants: a desire or a goal. However, action also includes things that happen *to* characters, or are involuntary, like Jo going into labour. This example shows that this term does not only describe highly physical aspects of a drama, such as Helen and Jo's chase around the flat. Some action will take place offstage (see below).

Backstory   the background story; what has happened in the past before the events that are played out over the course of the drama. It can be useful to know the key facts of a character's backstory – if they have one – and to think about how the past is relevant to the action of the play.

Costume   the clothes worn by actors to portray their character. Costumes can provide direct information about someone on stage, as with Jo's school uniform. Costumes often reflect when and where a play is set, and the class or social status of the characters.

Dialogue   the lines in a play that are spoken in a performance.

Direct address   an actor, on stage, speaking (or singing) to the audience directly.

Duologue   a conversation between two characters in a drama.

Monologue   a speech given by one character to one or more others. Monologues can appear as part of a duologue. It is quite common for a monologue to be important to the portrayal of a character. This is true of Helen; the audience learn about her childhood through her monologue in Act Two, Scene Two.

Narrative   The story of a play, as it is presented to an audience. A narrative includes what happens on stage, and events that are not actually dramatized by the playwright for the audience to see. For instance, Geof telling Helen that Jo is pregnant is part of the narrative, but it does not appear as part of the action.

Offstage   offstage action describes events of a play that are not performed, but that an audience learn about, and are asked to imagine: for example, Peter's affair. In the same way, offstage characters like Jo's father never actually appear, but are a (sometimes important) part of the narrative. Aim not to confuse 'offstage' with 'backstage'. This second term refers to the actual area in the theatre where actors go when they are not on the stage. It is part of the real world, rather than the fictional one of the play.

Playwright   author of a play, who you can also describe as a 'dramatist' (but *not* 'novelist'). Aim to spell this term correctly.

Props   props (short for 'properties') are the objects that actors use on stage during a performance. In *Honey*, they include a bottle of whisky, a broom and a newspaper. If you are not sure if something is a prop or part of a set, ask yourself if it could be held or carried in performance. If the answer is 'yes', it is most likely to be a prop. In addition to being functional, props can portray characters and themes.

Protagonist   the central character in a drama. Usually, protagonists are sympathetic (see below).

Scene a shorter sub-section of a play than an act, and usually (but not always) contained within one. As you can see by looking at the play text, scenes are often distinguished from one another by lapses of time, and/or changes in location or the particular characters on stage. Certain scenes will be memorable for the mood or atmosphere they create, or the themes explored within them. Sometimes, one scene will be made up of two or more shorter scenes. Because *Honey* is structured in this way, it is useful to tell your reader if you are focusing upon one particular *part* of a scene. For instance: 'In the second part of Act Two, Scene One, Jo is miserable about being pregnant.'

Set the way in which the fictional 'world' is represented on the stage, traditionally through a structure made of wood or metal that has been decorated, or 'dressed'. Other features of a set might include furniture, as in *Honey*. The set is often the first thing that an audience will see when they enter a theatre, and – like other visual components – can provide information about character and context.

Setting the 'where' and 'when' of the action; the 'world' of the play. For *Honey*, this is a cheap Salford flat in 1958. Whereas a set will be different in every new production of a play, its setting, decided by the playwright, will not change.

Sympathetic character a character that invites an audience's support, pity and sympathy (or empathy). An unsympathetic character is the opposite, and an audience may feel dislike towards them.

Additional terms

The following, additional terms have been explained elsewhere in this book (see Contexts and Drama technique).

- Dramatic form
- Episodic
- Linear

- Melodrama
- Music Hall
- New Wave
- Realism and kitchen sink realism, 'broken' and 'magnified' realism.

CHAPTER TWO

Behind the Scenes

There are three interviews in this section: with a director, an actor, and a teacher. You may find it useful to refer to the interview question if you discuss any one of these in class.

Bijan Sheibani (director)

Bijan Sheibani is a theatre director. In 2014, he directed the play at the Lyttleton, which is one of three performance spaces at the National Theatre in London. You can read an additional interview with him, and with the production's cast members, in the Background Pack.

Q1. Why do you think *A Taste of Honey* featured in the National Theatre's *100 Plays of the Century*?

I think Shelagh Delaney wrote this play with a strong desire to speak truthfully on behalf of a generation of women. If you watch her talking on the documentary that you can find on YouTube [*Shelagh Delaney's Salford*], I think you can see how unpretentious and articulate she is in the way she talks about growing up in Salford. What you get in *A Taste of Honey* is an authenticity, a huge swathe of feeling, and I think it's a play that still feels full of life because the human story is prioritized over any kind of political intent, or intention to shock, or be original, or any of the other pressures that get in the way of articulating experience truthfully.

Q2. Yours is one of several mainstream productions to have taken place in the last ten years. What attracted you to direct the play, and why do you think it continues to be popular?

My mother's family are from the North West of England, and I spent the first seven years of my life growing up in Liverpool, so these voices were very familiar to me. My uncle has a business in machinery parts in Salford. I'd never been there, but it was a place that was often talked about in our family. And I find it very funny. Comforting to read, because I recognize the wit, the banter, the dynamics between the characters. I think it captures a world that many people relate to.

Q3. When the play was first staged in the late 1950s, some reviewers were offended by it. Do you think it still has the capacity to shock audiences?

I don't find any of it shocking. I just thought, there it is, that's real, I believe that. I believe she'd do that, or he'd do that. And that's such a rare experience in the theatre. I don't know why, but it is, and that's one of the difficulties of making theatre. I do find some of it very sad. The moment when Jo is left alone at the end of Act One for example, and the end when Helen comes back and sits with Jo and listens to the children up on the croft. I find those moments very sad, and they stay with me. I have been asked whether I think Helen comes back at the end. I don't know. Probably. But she probably doesn't stick around for long, does she? I mean, will she be a good grandma? No. Will she be a fun grandma at some points? Yes. Definitely. She'll miss several birthdays, but then turn up with the best present — the one your mum refused to buy you. She's that kind of relative. There's no black and white in the characterization. Who doesn't love it when Helen turns up again in Act Two even though we know she's a bad mum? And

Jo knows how to handle her by the end. I don't worry about Jo. I think she'll be a good mum. Good enough anyway.

Q4. Professor Elaine Aston has described the play as 'broken realism' (Aston 2007: ix), because its realist elements are 'broken up' by non-realist ones: for instance, dancing between scenes and use of direct address. Can you comment on the decisions involved in staging a text of this type?

I think that Joan Littlewood and the original actors had quite a lot to do with the dancing and the direct address to the audience. Any text evolves through rehearsals, and in ours we discarded the direct address as it worked better for us to have them just talking to themselves like my Nan did, and we were ready not to do the dancing, but we just thought, why not, when the [jazz] music of the era is so good, you do just want to dance to it, and they're such vibrant people, Helen loves a good dance, so why shouldn't she? And why shouldn't Jo too? It became part of the fun of it, and a celebration of the characters, and the play and the era. And the sailor is such a romantic, he's bound to come in and sweep her off her feet, so the dancing for us was a must.

Q5. It will be important for the readers of this book to consider the play as something to be performed. What would be your advice to students who are not be able to see a live production of it?

It's always good to hear it read. Or to try and do it on its feet, so if you can't see it, try and make your own version!

Sally Lindsay (actor)

Sally Lindsay is an actor and presenter. She played Helen in a 2008 production at Manchester's Royal Exchange Theatre.

Q1. What attracted you to the role of Helen in the Royal Exchange production?

It was very special to me because the first thing I ever saw was at the Royal Exchange, which informed what I wanted to do for a living. I think *A Taste of Honey* is a very important play. It's sort of a blueprint for Mancunian art, and for northern art, because, without it, there would be no *Coronation Street*, there would be no *EastEnders*, there would be no working-class people on the television. If Shelagh Delaney had not drawn this picture of what actually happens to the working-class — what they have to put up with, what their fears and joys are — we'd still be looking at people walking through French windows and talking about what Daddy was going to buy them. That one play changed the face of British theatre in my view.

Doing it as a Mancunian actress was a very proud moment for me. Every single seat was sold every single night: it was almost like Manchester was waiting for it — saying, 'this is us, our culture, we own this play' — it was a very special moment. The poster we had was based on the [picture of] Morrissey outside Salford Lads' Club.[1]

Q2. Did the fact that you are from Manchester influence your approach to Helen?

I think it was intrinsic in me. The whole Mancuian thing informed [what I did]: I knew the streets, I knew the back alleys, I knew the cobbles; all those thing were very familiar.

Helen would have saved her make-up for going to the pub. That's what my Gran used to do; it was post-war. So you literally didn't wear any make-up [at home]. When Helen wanted to go singing, and get drinks off men, and take one

---

[1] Morrissey was a member of The Smiths, and influenced by Delaney (see 'Contexts'). Stephen Wright's photograph of the band outside the Club appeared on the inside cover of their 1986 album *The Queen is Dead*.

back, that's when she'd look fantastic. When I see productions of *A Taste of Honey* and Helen is this complete glamour puss at the start . . . that would not have happened and it drives me mad, and that's because of where I'm from. When we did the first scene [of the play], we walked in, pushing a pram, with all our crap in it, and I didn't have a scrap of make-up on, brown dress, brown coat, hair pinned up, nothing fancy. When [Helen] goes out with her fancy fella, she looks absolutely the best she possibly can, and is brilliant at that.

Q3. In a 2008 interview with *This is Lancashire*, you said you were working hard to make people 'not hate Helen'. Why did you think this was important?

Helen's quite a hard character; she's sort of had to be. She's survived. At the end of the day, she didn't leave Jo in an orphanage; however much she dragged her up, *she dragged her up*: she never left her. So, for that alone, I didn't want the audience to hate her. There's a very profound scene at the end when she's holding Jo [during her labour] and saying that everything's going to be alright, and that's when Helen finally reflects on why she's like she is: because she was deserted, she was abandoned. [This is during the monologue in which Helen remembers her own childhood.] She can't give the nurturing love that I give to my children – because I had that off my mother – as she never had that off her mother. She's done her absolute best with Jo, and that's what I wanted people to see. Sometimes, Helen is [performed as] very brash and two-dimensional: 'I'm a tart and I don't care.' I didn't see that; I saw this quite vulnerable child, almost in arrested development. She's never been grown-up enough to be a mother, and it's almost like Jo's the mother.

Q4. What was especially memorable or original about the way in which the Royal Exchange took the play from page to stage?

With the music, instead of a jazz band, [director] Jo Combes had a Mancunian DJ; we used Mancunian popular music. The

Smiths was very prominent, because Morrissey was obsessed with Shelagh Delaney. There was one point at which it was Joy Division, *Love Will Tear Us Apart*. When Helen finds out Jo's pregnant, and comes to give her money, I was wearing this amazing coat – dripping with money – and I came back in, and it was to the beat of that music. I wanted to audience to think, 'Leave them; they're fine; don't come back and ruin everything' and I remember that I could *feel* them go 'Oh my god' when I walked in. Because it was my face and Jodie (McNee's) [as Mancunian actors], and that music, it wasn't just this iconic play anymore, it turned into something very real, very recognizable for Manchester, and the audience were very engaged; because of the space of the Royal Exchange as well. You could feel people going: 'Oh no, she's back. Don't come back.'

There was some amazing stuff where you almost thought that her and Jo were bonding, then Helen always manages to mess it up. Helen sings in the first scene; I chose *A Nightingale Sang in Berkeley Square* [made famous by singer Vera Lynn in 1940], which was a popular song, then. I was performing this big song, and Jo's getting really into it, and they both seem quite happy, and then Helen turns around and just undercuts her [by saying 'You can't sing, can you?' (36)]. That's it: Jo's confidence is gone. They're still the closest thing to each another that they've got; that's why the last speech [about Helen's past] is so important.

We cut the 'blackbird' line at the end because the older audiences used to laugh along like it was normal, and the younger audiences used to be so horrified, some would walk out: the racism of it. We made the very tough decision to cut that, because it was detracting from everything else we had achieved. However racist everyone was (it's the way things were) — however racist Helen was — she would be the one who would walk in the park with that baby, and she would be strong enough to go, 'Come on then, what are you going to say?' The way the audience responded [to the 'blackbird' line] made out that Helen was just racist, putting the character down in a way.

Q5. Helen and Jo's relationship is obviously complex. Could you tell me something about developing it in rehearsal?

We came up with a timeline, which included how old I was [as Helen] when I had Jo, and what decisions I made. Her age when she had her [mid-twenties] probably informed her decision to keep her, and is why she wasn't taken off her. I think that was an important thing in the relationship, because she sort of looked at this baby as if to say, 'It's your fault I'm not out in the pub all night. You've made me grow up too quickly.' But then, Helen's never had the love that she wanted. It's that massive dichotomy of 'I resent you, but I love you, because you're the only thing I've ever had.' I wanted to put a bit of that in: '[Jo] is mine; I own this; no-one can take this away from me'; but also, 'I want to go to the pub and I can't'. We were sure she did go to the pub, when the baby was asleep; we imagined her shoving whisky in the [baby's milk] bottle, to knock her out. And I think that informed their relationship, and the fact that Helen literally dragged Jo around parts of Salford where she can get somewhere to live: and she always manages to find somewhere! They've never slept rough.

Krista Carson (teacher)

Krista Carson is an English, History and Media Studies teacher at Soham Village College in Cambridgeshire. She has taught the play for two years to GCSE students.

Q1. What attracted you to teaching *A Taste of Honey*?

After teaching *An Inspector Calls* and *A View from the Bridge* during the first few years of my teaching career, I picked up a copy of *A Taste of Honey* in an attempt to find some variety. The themes of uneasy mother–daughter relations, teenage love and pregnancy, and homosexuality, struck me as topics that would interest the most jaded twenty-first century teen!

Q2. How have your students responded to this play?

Interestingly, the best English Literature results of my teaching career came from the [first] group to which I taught *A Taste of Honey*. With that group, 98 per cent of students achieved or surpassed their target grades! The students really engaged with the play, much more than I've seen students engage with other contemporary texts. The main thing they enjoyed was the content; it was something they could relate to, something that, despite being written in the 1950s, is still relevant today. Issues like homosexuality, teenage pregnancy, bad relationships with parents, growing up ... these issues still exist today. I think they found it interesting and funny; for example, boys and girls alike enjoyed the relationship between Helen and Jo. Many discussions were had about the 'banter' they had, their 'role reversal' in terms of parenting, and how Jo was, ironically, following in the steps of the mother she claims to hate.

They also loved that Helen was described as a 'semi-whore'. The way each character is depicted, they way they speak and interact, makes them much more memorable to students who need to memorize characters, themes and quotes for exams. It's hard to confuse characters in a play like *A Taste of Honey* because they're all unique.

The boys I've taught have also taken issue with how men are presented in the text, which has provided a number of great discussion opportunities. A lot of time was spent discussing male–female relations in the text, comparing those to contextual and current views on relationships.

Q3. Do you think the issues portrayed in the play are still relevant, then, almost sixty years later?

We still have issues with homophobia, interracial relationships, teenage pregnancy, parent–children relationships, and poverty. The text provides an easy way to make contextual links between past and present, which is becoming increasingly important in mark schemes.

Q4. What do you find that students find most challenging about approaching this play?

To an extent, I think the reading of plays themselves is somewhat foreign to students. There is usually an initial period of confusion between prose and play-scripts. I often find students referring to 'the book' in their written analysis of themes [which should be avoided]. While they will have had access to Shakespeare, most of the students will have had very little experience reading contemporary plays that provide interesting insights into the period in which they were produced.

Students also initially struggle with understanding why Helen would be so angry that the baby might be black. There's always a good discussion about whether or not the baby's skin colour caused Helen to desert Jo for good or not. The ending is very ambiguous, and provides for great discussion. It does require a lot of historical context though, including an exploration of racial attitudes at the time versus those we experience today. Most students don't feel that the average person would react the way Helen does, so it takes some understanding of context to understand her motives.

Q5. What advice do you have for GCSE English Literature students writing about drama?

I usually try to teach my students to think like a director. If they were going to direct a version of the play, what advice would they give to actors? How would they approach specific scenes? This allows them to explore the way the playwright has ordered the text [and think about] how this affects the meaning conveyed. Structure is a big part of a play.

The playwright has to use dialogue to build setting, characterization and plot. Information is [often] revealed to the audience through words; as such, we spend a lot of time exploring the language used. I often work with small quotes, getting students to identify a key word within the quote, exploring its effect on the sentence, or even scene, as a whole. This gets them to view what's said in more detail, focusing on what it adds to character or plot development. Asking students to create a performance of the characters going on *The Jeremy Kyle Show* is always quite fun.

Things to do

1 What are the differences between Sheibani and Lindsay's views on (a) Helen's return in Act Two, and (b) Helen as a grandmother? Look at these two points separately, and decide with whom you most agree in each case. This could form the basis of a class debate.

2 Identify differences between the two productions of the play discussed in this section (2008 and 2014). This could involve looking at newspaper reviews, photographs of performances and the theatres themselves, as well as both the National Theatre Background Pack and Royal Exchange Production Pack (available at http://www. royalexchange.co.uk/65-a-taste-of-honey-resource-extra/ file).

3 As a class, use Carson's idea to improvise *The Jeremy Kyle Show* with the play's characters as guests. Give your episode a title, such as: 'My Sailor Boyfriend Disappeared . . . Now He's Back and Wants His Baby'; 'My Teenage Daughter's a Local Disgrace'; 'My Best Friend's Mother Came Between Us'. Members of the 'audience' should represent a varied 1950s society, and have the chance to ask questions. You may wish to repeat the same episode with a contemporary 'audience', then compare and contrast the two versions.

4 Write a diary entry from the point of view of Helen, either when she first discovered she was pregnant with Jo, or when she was a child herself.

CHAPTER THREE

Writing About the Play

This section of the book outlines techniques to help you apply your knowledge and understanding of the play to the final assessment. Whatever the examination question on *A Taste of Honey*, there are four areas in which you will be assessed. These focus on your ability to:

1   Produce a *personal response*: that is, an answer that contains your own ideas and opinions. At the same time, your response must be *critical* and *informed*, showing a thorough knowledge of the play, and a careful, academic approach to it. It is crucial that you provide clear *evidence* to illustrate and prove your ideas by making focused references to the text itself, or others related to it. This will include quoting from the play.

2   Analyse Delaney's use of *language*, *structure* and *form* (which includes dramatic techniques), in terms of the *meanings* that they create, and the *effects* they produce. Focusing on how the text has actually been written or constructed, and not just on what happens, will help you to write an essay that is analytical rather than descriptive.

3   Highlight links between the play and its *historical context* (the period in which it was written and first performed). These connections should be made where

relevant throughout your essay, not contained in a separate paragraph.

4   Write in a *formal* style, with accurate grammar, spelling and punctuation, and with an appropriate range of vocabulary (including English literature and drama terminology).

Obviously, these four things overlap. For example, relevant, accurate references to context will help to make your personal response an informed one. For this reason, the guidance that follows is not broken down according to the four areas of assessment. Instead, it outlines a series of key ways in which you can achieve your potential across all of them.

Personal response and different interpretations

The differences between the live productions of *Honey* that are mentioned in this book highlight that, like other works of literature, drama is open to interpretation. This is true on an academic level as well as a practical one: it applies to you, as someone studying it, just as it would to a theatre director deciding how to stage it. This does not mean that any view you have about the play is necessarily going to be valid, or that you can put forward any claim on the basis that it is your opinion. It *does* mean that you can have a different perspective from someone else in your class and neither of you will necessarily be 'wrong'. In fact, there is no reason why two opposing viewpoints cannot form the basis of two successful essays.

The following samples of analysis interpret one moment in the play in contrasting ways.

Analysis A
Helen is portrayed as an unsympathetic character when she follows Peter out of the flat at the end of Act Two, Scene One.

Although Jo does not want her to be there, this is an example of how Helen puts her relationships with men before her daughter, something an audience would know Helen has done throughout Jo's childhood by this stage in the play. Visually, Helen's act of leaving echoes her exit with Peter to go on honeymoon in Act One, which is important in showing her neglectfulness. It is actually only when Peter forces Helen to move out of his house, and she has no other choice, that she moves back into the flat. This demonstrates that Helen's concern for Jo is limited.

Analysis B

A more sympathetic side to Helen is portrayed at the end of Act Two, Scene One, just before she follows Peter out of the flat. Helen only leaves because Jo rejects her: saying 'No, thanks' (104) to her offer of staying. As soon as Peter leaves, Helen says, 'I'll . . . I'll . . . would you sooner I stayed here with you?' (104). This line shows that she is facing a dilemma because her usually articulate manner is replaced by a repeated word, and ellipses, which indicate a struggle to know what to say and do. This shows that she does care about Jo and is reluctant to leave her.

You may have noticed that different *types* of evidence have been used to support each of these analyses: for 'A', facts about the characters' actions and histories; for 'B', the language of the scene itself. You can read more about using different types of evidence in the following section.

If you develop a new, original or unusual interpretation of the play, talk it through with your teacher. They will be able to tell you whether or not your ideas have potential, and explain why in either case.

Evidence

Evidence is one of the most important ideas explored in this Guide. Using evidence effectively to support your written argument will be crucial to achieving your potential in the examination. The sub-sections that follow explore ways to apply evidence, and key forms that it takes in drama. Additional advice on using quotations is contained in a later, separate section.

Show, don't tell

Imagine a lawyer in a courtroom arguing that the woman in the dock is guilty, because she left her hat behind at the scene of the crime. The jury would expect to see the hat, and — if the lawyer did not have it — the jury would not necessarily believe him/her. In the same way, if you simply *tell* your reader your ideas about the play, it will be very difficult for you to produce a convincing argument. Instead, aim to *show* each of your key points: as clearly as if you were stood next to your reader, with an open copy of the play text, and could point at, say, a particular scene or line. Compare and contrast these examples (you will *not* need to provide page numbers for quotations):

1   Telling: Helen shows a lack of maternal care for Jo.
2   Showing: When Jo accidentally burns herself on a light bulb in the first scene, Helen's lack of maternal care is shown in her reaction: 'Wouldn't she get on your nerves?' (31).

You will notice that the second of these is far more convincing than the first.

Types of evidence

There are various different types of evidence that you can use in your essay, as reflected in the differences between sample analyses A and B (above). Taking advantage of a range of approaches will best enable you to explore the meanings and effects of language, structure and dramatic form, as well as express your ideas about character, theme and narrative.

Although some quoting is *always* essential, you will not necessarily use all of the techniques outlined below. Indeed, the type of evidence you use will depend upon the essay question. Your teacher will advise you on this when you are discussing examination technique and writing practice essays.

Dialogue

The play's spoken language is a key source of evidence, and something that you will almost certainly quote in your essay. Although you are likely to make use of some complete lines of dialogue, bear in mind that *parts* of a line and single words — sometimes from different parts of the play — can also support your claims. For example:

> Homophobic attitudes, which were more common in the 1950s, are represented through Helen and Peter's insults of Geof. 'Mary' (100), 'fruitcake parcel' (103) and 'pansified little freak' (97) are terms they use to describe him.

It will be important for you to consider not only what is said, but *how* things are written to be said in a performance. This will help you to appreciate the full, accurate meaning of the dialogue, and (possible) effects on an audience. The structure of individual sentences, and punctuation, can provide key information to help with this. Here are two examples:

> Delaney uses short sentences to portray Helen's shocked reaction to Jo's engagement: 'Well, you silly like bitch.' and 'I could choke you.' (70). By differing from how she usually speaks, these lines show a change in Helen's mood, highlighting to the audience that she is truly angry and worried.

> In the first scene, incomplete rhetorical questions in Helen's lines show her frustration with Jo. When Jo asks of the stove, 'It looks a bit ancient. How do I light it?', Helen replies, 'How do I – with a match' (32). Helen's lack of

patience could make an audience feel annoyance at the mother, and sympathy for the daughter, especially as Jo is attempting to make coffee for them both.

Some punctuation marks are used to create multiple different meanings and effects. For instance, compare and contrast these extracts, each of which contains at least one exclamation mark:

1   '[. . .] Oh! my head. [. . .] What a journey!' (35) (Helen in Act One, Scene One.)

2   'We're bloody marvellous!'(82) (Geof in Act Two, Scene One.)

3   'Let me get hold of her! I'll knock her bloody head round!' (96) (Helen in Act Two, Scene One.)

You may have observed that, in extract 1, exclamation marks are used to emphasize Helen's tendency to be melodramatic. By contrast, Delaney uses the same punctuation to create a mood of optimism in the first scene between Jo and Geof (extract 2). The final extract is one of many that contributes to an atmosphere of confrontation, with the exclamation mark suggesting a line that is either shouted or spoken with emotional intensity. The dissimilarities between these examples show how one punctuation mark can be used in several ways. As an individual or pair activity, you may wish to explore the different meanings and effects that stem from Delaney's use of other forms of punctuation, including question marks, dashes and ellipses.

   Finally, when you are using dialogue to back up a point, aim to remember that just because a character says something (about another character, for example), it does not automatically mean that it is true and can be used as reliable evidence. The following questions will help you assess the worth and validity of claims that characters make.

1   Is what they say confirmed by the events of the play?
    For example: Jo's descriptions of being neglected as a child are confirmed by Helen's actions.

2   Is there any reason to trust/distrust the character? For
     example: Geof is portrayed as selfless and honest, so
     what he says is trustworthy. Although Helen does not
     lie, she is prone to exaggerating. Therefore, it is
     possible that what she says about Jo's father is not
     completely accurate. An audience is encouraged to
     think this through the scepticism Geof expresses to Jo
     about Helen's story.

3   Is what they say likely to be true, given the historical
     context? For example: it is possible to believe Jo's
     suggestion that Geof was evicted from his flat for being
     gay, as homosexuality was illegal at this time. Her
     claim is further supported by action (the fact he moves
     into the flat).

Stage directions

Like dialogue, some stage directions are likely to be quoted in
your final essay. This can show your understanding of *how*
certain things should be staged, spoken, or happen, when the
play is performed.

Stage directions have a kind of double role in establishing a
play's setting and set. Try not to confuse these terms: setting
refers to the fictional 'world' of a play; set, to the actual way in
which this is represented on a stage. In terms of *Honey*'s
setting, one of the things stage directions do is to represent
parts of a city that is offstage (that is, that the audience does
not see): for instance, through '*fairground music*' (76). If you
are writing about ways that Delaney creates mood and
atmosphere, be mindful of the offstage elements detailed in
stage directions, as well as in the dialogue.

Stage directions about characters almost always describe
some sort of action, and can be used to illustrate certain things
about them. For instance, in Act Two, Scene One, Jo '*flings
herself down on the couch*' (88). This evidences her unsettled
state: the verb 'flings' suggests a melodramatic movement that

represents Jo's moodiness. The language of stage directions is as significant as that of the dialogue, as this example shows. Your opinions about characters' relationships with one another might also be supported through reference to stage directions. For example:

> For his second appearance in the play, Peter appears *'carrying a large bouquet and a box of chocolates and looking uncomfortable'* (56). The gifts and the size of the bouquet reinforce his wealth. His 'uncomfortable' expression reflects his anxiety about seeing Jo — who was rude and unwelcoming during his first visit — now that Helen has agreed to marry him. The chocolates are for Jo, reinforcing that he is concerned about her reaction to him.

Stage directions are also important to a play's dramatic form and techniques. The following two analyses demonstrate this.

> The opening stage directions highlight the play's form as kitchen-sink realism. The action takes place in a *'flat'* (29), which is an everyday, domestic interior. The fact it is *'comfortless'* hints at the characters' poverty, and working-class status, and the setting of *'Manchester'* (29), as a real place, suggests that the action will be realist.

> After the first onstage meeting between Jo and Boy, Helen *'dances on to the music, lies down and reads an evening paper'* (53). As soon as Jo appears, in the flat, Helen comments that she is 'a bit late' (53) in arriving home. This line, and the fact that she is reading a paper, indicate that the audience should imagine she has been in the flat for some time. Therefore, Helen's entrance, through dance, is not part of the main, realist action of the play. It highlights the fact that the form of realism is sometimes interrupted. An audience could be struck by the contrast between the dancing, and the more everyday act of reading a newspaper.

Action

There is, of course, an overlap between action and stage directions. However, it is possible to refer to what happens in the play more broadly to support your argument. This could involve mentioning a singular event or moment, like Boy proposing, or actions that repeat or form part of a pattern, like Helen's drinking.

You will not necessarily use quotations for this type of evidence, but it should be handled with the same high degree of care. There is little point basing an action on a 'fact' that is wrong: for example, 'Jo wants Helen's attention in Act One, so she shows her her drawings.' The following questions will help you to focus on the key facts about any one thing that happens.

1   When does it take place: during the play, or in the past? *If your answer is 'in the future', it is* not *part of the drama, but your idea about what might happen next.*

2   If it is during the play, in which act and scene?

3   If it is during the play, is it onstage action (that the audience sees), or offstage action (such as Peter forcing Helen to move out of his house)?

4   Does it have important links to anything else that happens?

5   What is its significance to the play, and what might it make an audience think or feel? *Onstage action is more likely to produce a strong effect than offstage.*

Staging possibilities and past productions

This is an advanced type of evidence for which you refer to how something *could* be staged, or *has* been staged in a professional production, to support your argument. It is not necessary to use this type of evidence to produce a high-quality essay.

Exploring how a particular part of the drama *might* be performed can be an effective way of developing a personal response. At the same time, it is vital that any creative ideas are grounded in an academic approach, and do not contradict anything stated in the play text. The following analysis argues that the close of the play does not necessarily have to portray Helen negatively.

> The close of Act Two is likely to reinforce Helen's status as an unsympathetic character: especially for a contemporary audience who may well find her behaviour racist. However, if the actor playing the character spoke her last few lines in a quiet, monosyllabic voice, with little movement, and stood as if in a state of shock, this would create a different effect from a production of the play in which she was unsympathetic, excited and angry, and raised her voice at Jo, who is already suffering by being in labour. This calmer, quieter interpretation could highlight how taboo mixed-race children were in 1950s Britain, rather than making Helen's response seem like a strange one.

This analysis is effective because:

1 it shows awareness of a more conventional approach to the character of Helen (insensitive to Jo, unsympathetic);
2 it makes direct, accurate links to historical context, which is used to justify the idea;
3 it contains vocabulary to describe how Helen would look and sound, including *practical* details (such as the volume of her voice).

Under 'Set' in the 'Dramatic technique' section, you can read an analysis that uses past productions as evidence for a discussion about Delaney's unconventional portrayal of women (in relation to the position of the kitchen in two different sets). Online images and footage make it possible to do this sort of writing without necessarily having seen the play. However:

- References to past productions should include the year, and the name of the theatre and director.

- Check that your interpretation is also supported by the play text itself.

- If you do develop ideas based on about how the play has been *or* could be performed, discuss them with your teacher before the examination, and be mindful of the fact that whether you can include them in your essay will depend entirely on the question.

Using the right evidence

It is important that the evidence you use is actually capable of supporting your ideas. There is little use in quoting a line of dialogue, for example, if it cannot prove your point on its own (that is, without the context of the lines that come before or after it). This is why it can sometimes be useful to draw evidence from different scenes, which could involve a small number of one-word quotations, as outlined above, or references to separate facts or events. For instance:

> Helen's mention of the 'slaughterhouse' (34) and a 'coffin' (46) in Act One, and Jo's dead flower bulbs in Act Two, highlight the theme of death.

This sentence shows how using evidence does not mean including all possible proof, but a *selection* of it: Jo's dream about Helen, in Act One, has not been included, although it could have been. Proving your point does not mean writing down everything you can remember from the play that you think is relevant, but providing the best examples with care and confidence.

Quoting

As a highly effective means of 'showing' evidence, it will be necessary to quote the play in the examination. First, it is important to understand what quoting actually means: taking an extract of a text (in this case, the play) and putting it in another (your essay). Extracts of *Honey* only become quotations when they are used in your writing. Therefore, it is you — not Delaney or any of the characters — who is doing the quoting. The only exception to this is dialogue in the play that comes from other texts, such as extracts of songs and lines from *Othello*. You will notice that these are presented within inverted commas (' '). It is now more common to use single inverted commas for quotations, as has been done in this book.

Effective quoting often involves including the quotation as part of your sentence. For example:

1   Helen sarcastically claims to be a 'cruel, wicked woman' (38).

2   The age gap between Peter and Helen is highlighted by her comment: 'I'm old enough to be your mother' (43).

3   Boy admits to Jo, 'I couldn't remember what sort of hands you had [. . .]. I stood there like a damn fool trying to remember [. . .]' (49).

For number 1, several words that appear at the start of the line have not been quoted. This is because they are not necessary to demonstrate Helen's sarcasm, and leaving them out does not change Delaney's meaning. For number 2, the quotation is introduced by a colon (:). This is one way in which you can structure your sentences to convey your meaning, with your point contained in the first part, and your proof for it in the second. Number 3 is a more advanced type of quoting, and you will not necessarily use it. The use of ellipses in square brackets tells your reader that you have edited out (cut) some words and/or punctuation. This can be anything from a single word to a number of sentences. It allows you to include only the text that is relevant to your point (which, in this case, could be that Boy does not know Jo that well). As with leaving out words from the start or end of lines, this must not alter the meaning of the text. Crucially — in order for you to avoid writing an essay that is just descriptive — all quotations will be followed by some analysis. Aim to do this whenever you provide evidence, whether or not it is quoted.

If you can convey information through a quotation, you do not need to put it in your own words as well. Try to avoid repetition of this kind:

> Geof asks Jo if she would like a piece of cake: 'Do you want a piece of cake, Jo?' (114). This shows that he cares about her.

Instead, this should be expressed as:

> Geof asks, 'Do you want a piece of cake, Jo?' This shows that he cares about her.

The language you use to introduce dialogue can show your understanding of both its meaning and effects. If you were to use the word 'asks' appropriately, as in the last example, this would show that you are aware that what is being quoted is a question; similarly, the word 'sarcastically' (used above for quotation number 1) shows knowledge of Helen's tone of voice. Verbs, especially, are a quick way to illustrate your understanding of the dialogue. See if you can find lines that could be introduced using the verbs in this word bank:

Shouts	Screams	Exclaims	Admits
Confides	Claims	Announces	Snaps

Memorizing quotations can be challenging, and you may approach this differently from your peers. Effective techniques include memorizing lines, as actors do, which might involve rehearsing scenes with friends; displaying quotations in places that you see regularly, such as above your desk, or making and listening to a recording of them. If you find it hard to remember a quotation in the examination, simply do your best. An imperfect quotation could still provide evidence and is better than no quotation at all.

Approaching character

When you are writing about the characters, keep in mind that they are *fictional* constructs. Delaney's characters may reflect certain things about the realities of the 1950s, but they are not real themselves. Writing bullet points that outline the key facts about each character, including their backstories, can help with this: partly as a way of checking that you have not confused your own interpretation (or the opinion of other characters) with what actually happens. For instance, if your list of facts about Jo includes 'has a baby', it is not accurate.

It is crucial to see the facts of the play as unchangeable. 'If only Jo had not let Helen move back in' and 'It is a shame Peter took Helen away in Act One' are the sort of statements to avoid. These suggest that the events of the play could have turned out differently, as if they had happened in real life. Instead, your task is to consider the significance of the action, exactly as Delaney presents it.

Moral judgements about the characters, such as praising or criticizing them, should also be avoided. This can be difficult, especially if you have an emotional reaction to the play. You will notice that the analysis of Helen, under 'Character', largely outlines ways in which she is presented as being different from an 'ideal' mother, and how this relates to historical context. By contrast, 'Helen deserved to be kicked out by Peter' is an example of the sort of judgemental claim that you should not make in academic writing. Of course, analysing how an audience might react to a character is something you can and should do, where relevant. For instance: 'Because of her treatment of Jo, it is unlikely that an audience would pity

Helen when her marriage to Peter breaks down.' This shows understanding of Helen as an unsympathetic *character*, and justifies the audience's (likely) reaction on the basis of facts about her relationship with Jo.

Finally, aim to have an understanding of the characters' status. This means being aware of who is the most and least powerful character at any given point in the play, and considering the relevance of this to the meaning of the scene more generally. You will notice that status relationships can change over the course of a drama; Jo and Helen each try, repeatedly, to make themselves of a higher status than the other! Moreover, a character's status is determined by the type of real person, or identity, they represent. For instance, Geof's homosexuality is a reason that he has a lower status than Helen and Peter.

Historical context

Plays, like novels, and other sorts of art, reflect the historical context in which they were produced. In the examination, it will be necessary for you to show you understand this idea, and illustrate particular ways in which it applies to the play. Apart from the 'Contexts' section, you might have noticed that, over the course of this book, historical context has been referred to *as* and *when* it is relevant. For instance, the character of Boy and Jo's relationship with him has been linked to racial tensions in Britain during the fifties. Certain parts of the play, like this, have stronger or more obvious connections with context than others. Your task is to look for opportunities, while *planning* your essay, to connect the play to its context: not produce one paragraph explaining all you know about 1950s Britain, or try to include some historical information for every single point that you make. To do this successfully, be aware of the fact that contextual information is not separate from the drama, but an important way in which its meanings can be understood. For instance, knowing that music hall had been a popular type of entertainment in the decades leading up to the 1950s helps to understand its influence on the play's form. This example shows how context is not just important to the plot, themes and characters, but to dramatic technique. Finally, remember that a play is a work of fiction, even when it represents real places or people. It *reflects* certain things about its context, but cannot be used as proof of historical fact.

Essay structure

Think of the points you put forward in an essay as part of a chain of evidence that make up one argument. The essay should open with a short introduction, to give an overview, and close with a conclusion that briefly relates your main ideas back to the question. Clearly presented paragraphs should be used to group related ideas together. Introduce your new area of focus clearly to your reader at the start of each. Every individual point you make should be expressed fully and carefully, with relevant evidence, before you move on to the next.

Writing style

In the examination, it will be necessary for you to write in formal, standard English. This can be challenging: especially as you will be quoting dialogue that contains slang, incomplete sentences and other aspects of conversational English that are not 'formal' at all! Remember that your own style should be different from that of the play. To achieve this:

1   **Be as clear as possible in expressing your ideas.** Writing formally does not mean in a style that is difficult to understand. Avoid long, run-on sentences that contain lots of ideas; a short sentence can be highly effective and help give your work clarity. Use language carefully, such that the reader knows exactly what you are

referring to. For instance, in a play about two women, the word 'she' should be used very carefully to avoid confusion. It is better to repeat character names than to risk being unclear.

2   **Use formal language and be direct.** For instance, refer to Helen as Jo's 'Mother' rather than informal variations (like 'Mum' or 'Mam'). If you are writing about one of the play's potentially more embarrassing topics, such as sex, be direct. Stating that 'Jo and Boy have sex over Christmas' is preferable to writing something vague, like 'they became intimate', or a crude alternative.

3   **Use terminology accurately, but avoid definitions.** Simply writing 'The duologue between Helen and Jo is heated in this scene', for example, *shows* that you understand what a duologue is. A sentence after that giving a definition would be unnecessary.

4   **Write in the present tense** when you are referring to events that take place in the play; anything that happened in the past (like Helen's affair with Jo's father) should be expressed in the past tense, as, of course, should information about historical context. This approach has been taken in this book.

5   **Practise and prepare** as best you can, being aware of any particular areas that you find difficult. If punctuation is something you find challenging, for example, set aside short, regular periods to develop this skill, and take advantage of the support that your teacher will offer you.

In the examination

It can be tempting to start writing as soon as possible after the examination begins. However, setting aside time to read the question carefully, plan, and check, your work, is very important.

You may also wish to write down any relevant key quotations, or historical facts, before you start writing. Planning efficiently means that — when you do start writing — you will already know what all of your key areas of focus (or paragraphs) are, and that all of them definitely contribute to answering the question. You may have developed an interest in, or an excellent idea about, an aspect of the play that is not relevant to the question. In this case, it is important that you resist including it.

Leaving time to proofread your work will allow you to check that what you *intended* to write is matched by what you have *actually* written. You may find that you change minor parts of your answer to make your response as clear as possible for your reader. Avoid panicking towards the end of an examination, and adding an extra paragraph that was not part of your plan. If this does not contribute to your argument, it can undermine the quality of everything else you have done.

Examinations can, of course, be stressful experiences. Rather than focusing on this endpoint while you are studying *A Taste of Honey*, aim to take advantage of opportunities for discussion, performance, debate and research: both in and out of your English classroom. Not only will this help you to fulfil your academic potential, but make this aspect of your studies a rich and rewarding one.

BIBLIOGRAPHY

Anon. (2008) 'A Taste of Honey Production Pack'. Royal Exchange Theatre Education: Resource Extra [online]. Available at: http://www.royalexchange.co.uk/65-a-taste-of-honey-resource-extra/file [accessed: 16 October 2015].

Anthony, Andrew (2014) 'Lesley Sharp Interview'. *The Guardian* [online]. Available at: http://www.theguardian.com/culture/2014/feb/08/lesley-sharp-interview-taste-of-honey [accessed: 16 October 2015].

Aston, Elaine (2008) 'Foreword' in Elaine Aston and Glenda Leeming (eds) *Shelagh Delaney: A Taste of Honey*. London, Bloomsbury, v–ix.

Billington, Michael (2007) *State of the Nation: British Theatre since 1945*. London, Faber and Faber.

Delaney, Shelagh (1959) ITN interview [online]. Available at: https://www.youtube.com/watch?v=SM22loR53TQ [accessed: 16 October 2015].

Delaney, Shelagh (2016 [1959]) *A Taste of Honey*. London, Bloomsbury.

Derby Theatre (2014) 'A Taste of Honey — What Did You Think?' Derby Theatre and Hull Truck Theatre [online]. Available at: https://www.youtube.com/watch?v=OfYwH1NHQ6k [accessed: 16 October 2015].

Esche, Edward J. (1994 [1992]) 'Shelagh Delaney's *A Taste of Honey* as Serious Text: A Semiotic Reading' in Adrian Page (ed.) *The Death of the Playwright?*, Basingstoke, Macmillan, 67–81.

Eyre, Richard and Wright, Nicholas (2000) *Changing Stages: A View of British Theatre in the 20th Century*. London, Bloomsbury.

Goring, Edward (1958) Review of *A Taste of Honey* at the Theatre Royal, Stratford, *Daily Mail*, 28 May 1958.

Harding, John (2014) *Sweetly Sings Delaney*. London, Greenwich Exchange.

Ince, Ola (2014) 'National Theatre Learning: *A Taste of Honey*
    Background Pack'. London, The Royal National Theatre Board
    [online]. Available at: http://www.nationaltheatre.org.uk/
    document/a-taste-of-honey-background-pack [accessed: 16
    October 2015].

Kerr, Jennifer (ed.) (2013) '*A Taste of Honey* — trailer'. Hull Truck
    Theatre [online]. Available at: https://vimeo.com/57050765
    [accessed: 16 October 2015].

Kitchin, Laurence (1960) *Mid-Century Drama*. London, Faber and
    Faber.

MacInnes, Colin (1959) 'A Taste of Reality' in *Encounter*, Issue 31,
    No. 67 (April), 70–71.

Pattie, David (2012) *Modern British Playwriting: the 1950s*.
    London, Methuen Drama.

Russell, Ken (1960) *Shelagh Delaney's Salford*. BBC Monitor series
    [online]. Available at: https://www.youtube.com/
    watch?v=iXmMsOBrx9g [accessed 16 October 2015].

Shulman, Milton (1958) Review of *A Taste of Honey* at the Theatre
    Royal, Stratford, *Evening Standard*, 28 May 1958.

Snow, Georgia (2015) 'Less than a third of new plays written by
    women, report finds'. *The Stage* [online]. Available at: https://
    www.thestage.co.uk/news/2015/less-third-new-plays-written-
    women-report-finds/ [accessed 16 October 2015].

Szreter, Simon and Fisher, Kate (2010) *Sex Before the Sexual
    Revolution: Intimate Life in England 1918–1963*. Cambridge,
    Cambridge University Press.

Taylor, John Russell (1963 [1962]) *Anger and After: a Guide to the
    New British Drama*. London, Pelican.

Wandor, Michelene (1987) *Look Back in Gender: Sexuality and the
    Family in Post-War British Drama*. London, Methuen.

Wandor, Michelene (2001) *Post-war British Drama: Looking Back
    in Gender*. London, Routledge.

INDEX